Herkimer County
Community College Library
Herkimer, New York
13350

1. Books may be kept for three weeks and may
be renewed once, except when otherwise noted.

2. Reference books, such as dictionaries and en-
cyclopedias are to be used only in the Library.

3. A fine is charged for each day a book is not
returned according to the above rule.

4. All injuries to books beyond reasonable wear
and all losses shall be made good to the satisfaction of the Librarian.

5. Each borrower is held responsible for all books
drawn on his card and for all fines accruing on
the same.

ESSAYS IN
THE HISTORY
OF RELIGIONS

ESSAYS IN THE HISTORY OF RELIGIONS

Joachim Wach

*Edited by Joseph M. Kitagawa
and Gregory D. Alles*

MACMILLAN PUBLISHING COMPANY
NEW YORK
Collier Macmillan Publishers
LONDON

Macmillan Publishing Company
866 Third Avenue, New York, NY 10022

Collier Macmillan Canada, Inc.

Library of Congress Catalog Card No.: 87-17187

Printed in the United States of America

printing number
1 2 3 4 5 6 7 8 9 10

The essays in this book originally appeared in the following publications:

"Master and Disciple: Two Religio-Sociological Studies," trans. by Suzi Heigl-Wach and Frederick J. Streng, *Journal of Religion* 42.1 (Jan. 1972): 1–21. Reprinted by permission of The University of Chicago Press.

"Mahāyāna Buddhism" trans. by Nancy Auer Falk from *Mahāyāna, besonders im Hinblick auf das "Saddharma-Pundarika-Sūtra."* Munich-Neubiberg: Schloss, 1925. Printed by permission of Nancy Auer Falk.

"Sociology of Religion," *Twentieth Century Sociology*, ed. by Georges Gurvitch and Wilbert E. Moore. New York: Philosophical Library, 1945, pp. 406–437. Reprinted by permission of Philosophical Library, Inc.

"Radhakrishnan and the Comparative Study of Religion." Reprinted from *The Philosophy of Sarvepalli Radhakrishnan*, ed. by Paul Arthur Schilpp, by permission of The Open Court Publishing Company, La Salle, Illinois. Copyright 1952 by The Library of Living Philosophers, Inc.

"On Teaching History of Religions," *Pro regno pro sanctuario*, ed. by W. J. Kooiman and J. M. van Veen. Nijkerk: G. F. Callenbach, 1950, pp. 525–532. Reprinted by permission of G. F. Callenbach bv.

"On Understanding," *The Albert Schweitzer Jubilee Book*, ed. by A. A. Roback. Cambridge, Mass.: Sci-Art Publishers, n.d. (1945), pp. 131–146.

Library of Congress Cataloging in Publication Data:

Wach, Joachim, 1898–1955.
 Essays in the history of religions / Joachim Wach ; edited by Joseph M. Kitagawa and Gregory D. Alles.
  p.   cm.
  Bibliography: p.
  Includes index.
  Contents: Master and disciple—Mahāyāna Buddhism—Wilhelm von Humboldt—Sociology of religion—Radhakrishnan and the comparative study of religion—Religion in America—On teaching history of religions—On understanding.
  ISBN 0-02-933520-5
  1. Religion—Study and teaching.   2. Religion and sociology.
 I. Kitagawa, Joseph Mitsuo, 1915- . II. Alles, Gregory D.
 III. Title.
 BL41.W33   1987
 291'.09—dc19   87-17187
                                                        CIP

To
Joachim Wach's students

Contents

INTRODUCTION

Joseph M. Kitagawa

SHORTLY AFTER Joachim Wach's death in the summer of 1955, I wrote "Joachim Wach, Teacher and Colleague" (*The Divinity School News* 22, no. 25 [Autumn 1955] [University of Chicago]); "A Glimpse of Professor Wach" (*Register* 45, no. 4 [November 1955] [Chicago Theological Seminary]); and "Joachim Wach et la Sociologie de la Religion" (*Archives de Sociologie des Religions* 1, no. 1 [Janvier-Juin 1956] [Paris]). I have also written about Wach in my introductions to three posthumous works: *The Comparative Study of Religions* (New York: Columbia University Press, 1958); *Understanding and Believing* (New York: Harper & Row, 1968); and *Introduction to the History of Religions* (New York: Macmillan, 1987). Readers may also consult the account of Wach's life and thought in *Classical Approaches to the Study of Religion*, 2 vols. (The Hague: Mouton, 1973) by Jacques Waardenburg.

Joachim Wach was born in 1898 in Chemnitz, Saxony, and died in 1955 while vacationing in Orselina, Switzerland. He was a descendant of Moses Mendelssohn, a lineage that affected his life and career both positively and negatively. His paternal grandfather, the noted jurisconsult Adolph Wach, married Lily, the daughter of Felix Mendelssohn, the composer. His father, Felix, married Kathe, granddaughter of the composer's brother, Paul. Young Wach was early exposed to music, literature, poetry, and both classical and modern languages.

After attending the Vitzshumsche Gymnasium in Dresden and spending two years in military service (1916–1918), Wach enrolled at the University of Leipzig, but in 1919 and early 1920 he studied with Friedrich Heiler at Munich and with Ernst Troeltsch at Berlin. He then returned to Leipzig to study Oriental languages and the history and philosophy of religion. For a time he came under the spell of the enigmatic poet Stefan George, whose writings spoke of a heightened sense of "experience," through which one perceives the multiple threads of the tapestry of life as a transparent whole. Wach received his Ph.D. degree in 1922 from Leipzig with a thesis entitled "The Foundations of a Phenomenology of the Concept of Salvation," published as *Der Erlösungsgedanke und seine Deutung* (1922).

When Wach started teaching at Leipzig in 1924, the discipline of the history of religions *(Religionswissenschaft)*, still in its infancy, faced serious dangers. On the one side, its right to exist was questioned by those who insisted that whoever knows one religion (i.e., Christianity) knows all religions; on the other, its religio-scientific methodology was challenged by reductionist psychological and social-scientific approaches. Thus in his habilitation thesis, *Religionswissenschaft: Prolegomena zu ihrer wissenschaftstheoretischen Grundlegung* (1924), Wach insisted on the integrity and autonomy of the history of religions, liberated from theology and the philosophy of religion. He emphasized that both historical and systematic dimensions are necessary to its task, and he argued that the discipline's goal was "understanding" *(Verstehen)*: "The task of *Religionswissenschaft* is to study and to describe the empirical religions. It seeks descriptive understanding; it is not a normative discipline. When it has understood the historical and systematic aspects of the concrete religious configurations, it has fulfilled its task"

(p. 68). His *Religionswissenschaft* is still regarded as a small classic in the field.

Wach's agenda centering on understanding led him to produce a three-volume work on the development of hermeneutics in the nineteenth century (*Das Verstehen*, 1926–1933). The first volume traced the hermeneutical theories of such major figures as Friedrich Schleiermacher, G. A. F. Ast, F. A. Wolff, August Boeckh, and Wilhelm von Humboldt. The second volume dealt with theological hermeneutics from Schleiermacher to Johannes von Hofmann, while the third volume examined theories of historical hermeneutics from Leopold von Ranke to historical positivism. Understandably, Wach felt it absolutely necessary to establish solid hermeneutical foundations for the history of religions.

Wach was convinced that the history of religions *(Religionswissenschaft)* should not lose its empirical character. He felt C. P. Tiele and P. D. Chantepie de la Saussaye had failed to make an adequate distinction between the history of religions and the philosophy of religion. He was critical both of those who started with philosophy and developed science and of those who started with science and moved toward philosophy. In his view, the history of religions lay, rather, precisely between the two. In this respect he followed Max Scheler, who posited a "concrete phenomenology of religious objects and acts" between a historical study of religions (a positive *Religionswissenschaft*) and the essential phenomenology of religion *(die Wesensphänomenologie der Religion)*. According to Scheler, this intermediate discipline aims at the fullest understanding of the intellectual contents of one or more religious forms and the consummate acts in which these intellectual contents have been given. It was Wach's conviction that an inquiry such as Scheler envisaged could be carried out only by employing the religio-scientific method of *Religionswissenschaft*.

Wach's reputation for erudition attracted many students to Leipzig. However, his productive career there came to an abrupt end in April 1935. The government of Saxony, under pressure from the Nazis, terminated Wach's university appointment on the ground of his Jewish lineage, even though his family had been Christian for four generations. Fortunately, through the intervention of American friends, Wach was invited to teach at Brown University in Providence, Rhode Island, where he stayed until 1945. His adjustment to the new environment was by no means easy; he was especially anxious about his mother, sister, and brother, who were suffering under the Nazi tyranny. From 1945 until his death, Wach taught at the University of Chicago.

Wach always asserted that the method of the history of religions must be commensurate with its subject matter, that is, the nature and expressions of the religious experience of humankind as that experience has been unfolded in history. Following his mentor, Rudolf Otto, Wach defined religious experience as the experience of the holy. Throughout his life, he never altered his views on the basic structure of the discipline: its twin tasks (historical and theoretical); the centrality of religious experience and its threefold expressions (theoretical, practical, and sociological); and the crucial importance of hermeneutics. But Wach emphasized three different methodological accents in three successive phases of his career.

During his first phase, Wach was preoccupied with the hermeneutical basis for the descriptive-historical task of the discipline. He was greatly influenced by the philological hermeneutics of August Boeckh, who defined the hermeneutical task as "re-cognizing" that which had previously been "cognized," that is, as articulating what has been recognized in its pristine character, even to the extent of "re-constructing" in its totality that which does not appear as a whole. Accordingly, Wach insisted that the historian of religions must first try to assimilate that which had been recognized as a religious phenomenon and "re-produce" it as one's own. Then he must observe and appraise that which has become one's own as an objective something apart from oneself.

During his second phase, Wach attempted to develop the systematic dimension of the history of religions by following the model of sociology. In Wach's view, the sociological (systematic) task of *Religionswissenschaft* had two main foci: (1) the interrelation of religion and society, which requires an examination, first, of the sociological roots and functions of myths, doctrines, cults, and associations, and, second, of the sociologically significant function and effect of religion in society; and (2) the study of religious groups. In dealing with religious groups, and especially with the variety of self-interpretations advanced by these groups, Wach employed the typological method. As he stated in his *Sociology of Religion* (1944), he was convinced of the need to develop a closer rapport between *Religionswissenschaft* and other disciplines, especially with the social and human sciences. In this sense, his *Sociology of Religion* was an an attempt to bridge "the gulf which still exists between the study of religion and the social sciences" (p. v). Yet the ultimate aim of his sociological (systematic) study of religion was "to gain new insights into the relations between the various forms of expression of religious experience and eventually to understand better the various aspects of religious experience itself" (p. 5).

During the third phase, Wach's concern for an integral understanding of the various aspects of religious experience and its expressions led him to reassess not only the relationship of *Religionswissenschaft* with the social sciences but also its relationship with normative disciplines such as philosophy of religion and the various theologies. After Wach's sojourn in India, where he delivered the Barrows Lectures at various universities in 1952, this concern became more pronounced. It was, in fact, one of the key motifs of his lectures on the history of religions sponsored by the American Council of Learned Societies in 1954. Increasingly the vocabulary of "explaining" *(Deuten; Erklären)* came to be used side by side with that of "understanding" *(Verstehen)* in his lectures. Wach shared his dream of pursuing a new grand synthesis for the study of the human religious experience, a sequel to earlier works such as *Religionswissenschaft* and *Das Verstehen*, with friends during the Seventh Congress of the International Association for the History of Religion, held in Rome in the spring of 1955. But death came that summer and robbed him of this venture.

When A. Eustace Haydon retired as professor of comparative religion at the University of Chicago, Wach agreed to take his place. There he spent the last ten years of his life, 1946 to 1955, as professor of the history of religions in the Divinity School (then part of the Federated Theological Faculty) and with the University of Chicago's Committee on the History of Culture.

When Wach arrived in Chicago, the university was not even sixty years old. William Rainey Harper, who founded the university in 1892, had counted among his close friends Rabbi Emil G. Hirsch, the first professor of rabbinical literature and philosophy; John Henry Barrows, pastor of the First Presbyterian Church and permanent chairman of the 1893 World's Parliament of Religions; and Mrs. Caroline E. Haskell, who donated to the university the Haskell Lectureship on Comparative Religion and the Haskell Oriental Museum. All were keenly interested in comparative religion, however that subject was understood, and so a foundation was well laid early on at Chicago for the tradition to which Wach found himself heir.

By the mid-1940s, in fact, Chicago had seen at least three major approaches to comparative religion. The first was epitomized by George Stephen Goodspeed (d. 1905), author of *A History of the Babylonians and Assyrians.* Goodspeed established the Department of Comparative Religion in the university's Division of Humanities and was himself professor of comparative religion and ancient history. That he clearly approached religion, or religions, through the Judeo-Christian tradition can be seen in the title of a small booklet he edited after the Parliament: *The World's First Parliament of Religions: Its Christian Spirit, Historic Greatness and Manifold Results* (Chicago: Hill & Shuman, 1895). Similarly, in a presentation delivered at the Haskell Oriental Museum, Goodspeed expressed the hope that "there will go forth from these halls [of the University of Chicago] enlightenment, inspiration, and guidance in that learning which has come from the East and West, culminating in the Book of Books and in the teachings of the Son of Man, [which] will ever abide as our most precious possession."[1]

The second approach to comparative religion at Chicago was advocated by George Burman Foster (d. 1918), who accepted a widely held three-layered scheme: (1) a narrow history of religions—conceived to be the simple historical study of "raw" religious data, often colored by an evolutionary ideology—toward (2) "comparative religion," which aims to classify religious data and culminates in (3) a philosophy of religion (or a theology) that provides a meaning for the comparative religion enterprise as a whole. Louis Henry Jordan, too, accepted this combination of "scientific study of religion" and "philosophy of religion" as the program of comparative religion.[2]

The third approach, spearheaded by A. Eustace Haydon (d. 1975), was in a sense a critique of and a reaction to the first and second orientations. An erudite scholar and an eloquent speaker, Haydon had outgrown the fundamentalist faith of his childhood, as is evident in his numerous writings. For him, the loss of his childhood orthodoxy had three important outcomes. First, religious reality had given way to the ethical and the aesthetic, to use Kierkegaardian shorthand, and he found a "home" for himself in the Ethical Culture movement. Second, he was driven to a religious relativism as the alternative to affirming Christian faith as the only religion of humankind's salvation. Third, he championed comparative religion, understood by him as an umbrella term for objective studies, by specialists, of the historic religious traditions, no more and no less.

Haydon took it for granted that, originally, human needs created all the forms of religion. Throughout history, all religions had had to wrestle with the problem of change or, if you will, the problem of "modernism"; yet, in the twentieth century the great historic religions were forced to come to terms with revolutionary forces heretofore unknown, namely, the "new scientific thinking" and "applied science." The former had profound implications for all aspects of human life, especially for traditional religions and their ancient cosmologies, theologies, and supernaturalisms. And applied science—especially modern machinery, communications, and systems of transportation—was already reshaping the face of the world. By way of responding to this new situation, Haydon, qua comparative religionist, organized the World Fellowship of Faiths in 1933. The conference dealt with Islam, Judaism, Christianity, Buddhism, Confucianism, and Hinduism and tried to generate discussion on four topics: (1) World-Religions and Modern Scientific Thinking; (2) World-Religions and Modern Social-Economic Problems; (3) World-Religions and Inter-Cultural Contacts; and (4) the Task of Modern Religion. Haydon was persuaded that the six religious systems all faced the same problems.[3]

The contrast between the 1893 World's Parliament of Religions, which helped to shape the first approach to comparative religion at Chicago, and the 1933 World Fellowship of Faiths, the brainchild of its third approach, is interesting. Both divorced religious realities from human communities, so that participants could speak, for example, of Buddhism apart from Buddhist community life; and both dealt with socioeconomic problems as if they owed nothing to religious factors. In contrast, though, to the 1893 conference, which recognized the importance of the past to various religions, the 1933 conference concerned itself solely with the modern phases and movements of the living world religions.

But by far the most salient feature of the 1933 conference was the way in which it equated both religion and morality and comparative religion and science. In the words of K. Natarajan of Bombay, "The task of religion in all ages has been to assert the supremacy of the moral law over the lives of individuals and nations."[4] And Haydon's friend, Rabbi Solomon Goldman, added: "The ancient techniques of prayer and ritual need to be retained only in so far as they are aesthetically appealing. Modern religion must become the friend and not the enemy of science."[5] Haydon agreed: the task of comparative religion was to help people overcome the anti-scientific bias and to show them the religion of tomorrow, a synthesis of science and idealism. "The whole world," he said, "wrestles with the same problems, aspires toward the same ideals, and strives to adjust inherited thought-patterns to the

same scientific ideas. In such times the prophetic fire of religious aspiration flames anew and religions move into new
embodiments . . . the religions of tomorrow are emerging
surrounded by a multitude of modernizations of the old."[6]
Ironically, it was Haydon, the ex-fundamentalist, who trans-
ferred the Department of Comparative Religion from the
Humanities to the Divinity School of Chicago shortly before
his retirement in 1944.

When Wach arrived in Chicago, he was aware that comparative religion at the university had had three successive
approaches, none of which appealed to him. In order to make
a fresh beginning, Wach proposed to refer to his enterprise
as the History of Religions *(Religionswissenschaft)*, which was
the official English designation of the international association.[7]
Wach was afraid that the name might suggest a purely historical
discipline, but he was more afraid that the history of religion,
in the singular, the usage he had preferred in Germany, might
suggest a philosophical discipline. Thus he settled on the
history of religions and used the term consistently for the
remainder of his career.

Wach was irenic by nature and wanted to relate himself
positively to each of the earlier orientations in comparative
religion. Accordingly, he paid special attention to (1) the special
place of Judaism and Christianity in Western civilization, which
the first approach had stressed; (2) the relationship between
the history of religions and philosophy of religion (or theology),
which the second approach had emphasized; and (3) the concern North Americans had shown for specific religious traditions, such as Hinduism, Buddhism, and Islam. (Wach la-
mented, however, the lack of interest in the so-called primitive
religions in North America).

When Wach came to the campus on the Midway, the
University of Chicago was an unusually exciting place under
the dynamic leadership of Robert Maynard Hutchins. During
the war years, the university made a point of welcoming
European refugee scholars—many from Germany; some, like
Enrico Fermi, from Italy—who helped to create an interna-

tional atmosphere at Chicago. The Divinity School, then under the deanship of the young theologian Bernard M. Loomer, was involved in creating the Federated Theological Faculty, which included Ernest Cadman "Pomp" Colewell, Amos Wilder, J. Coert Rylaarsdam, Allen P. Wikgren, Paul Schubert, Wilhelm Pauck, Charles Hartshorne, Bernard E. Meland, Daniel Day Williams, Sidney Mead, James H. Nichols, James Luther Adams, and Samuel Kincheloe. Wach took a modest room in the Disciples Divinity House, 1156 East 57th Street, and later moved to an apartment in the Ingleside Avenue faculty building. He was close to many scholars in the neighborhood, notably O. J. Matthijs Jolles, one-time chairman of the Committee on the History of Culture; Peter von Blankenhagen; Ludwig Bachhofer; Robert Platt; Robert Redfield; John Nef; Wilbur Katz; Everett Hughes; and his own cousin, Otto von Simpson. Wach also received many visitors who delighted his students by appearing in his classes. Among these visitors were Martin Buber, Gershom G. Scholem (Wach's fellow student at Munich), D. T. Suzuki, Hideo Kishimoto, Gerardus van der Leeuw, Jacques Duschesne-Guillemin, A. A. Fyzee, and Swami Vivekananda.

From the beginning, it was crystal-clear to Wach that he wanted to teach the history of religions (*Allgemeine Religionswissenschaft*), which is an autonomous discipline situated between normative studies, such as philosophy of religion and theology, and descriptive studies, such as sociology, anthropology, and psychology. He was also convinced that *Religionswissenschaft* consisted of two complementary aspects, the "historical" and the "systematic" procedures of study. The "historical" task required a mutual interaction between the "general" history of religions and the historical studies of "specific" religions, while the "systematic" task aimed at disciplined generalizations and the structuring of data and depended on a collaboration of phenomenological, comparative, sociological, psychological, and other studies of religions. Historical and systematic inquiries were to be thought of as two interdependent dimensions of one and the same discipline called the history of religions (*Religionswissenschaft*).

Wach affirmed that the history of religions should start with the historic religions. Thus he shared common ground with the third approach to comparative religion at Chicago. But unlike this third approach, he never accepted the premise that what authenticated, say, Hinduism or Buddhism is simply Hindu or Buddhist religious experience. Wach was convinced that the raison d'être of the history of religions is the hidden "religious experience" of humankind, described as the experience of the "holy" by Rudolf Otto and as the experience of "power" by G. van der Leeuw. Wach was sympathetic to the desire to find a special place in the study of religion for Judaism and Christianity, which was the emphasis of the first approach to comparative religion at Chicago. But, unlike the first approach, which viewed all religions through the window of the Jewish-Christian tradition, Wach insisted that Judaism and Christianity alike must be seen as parts of the "whole" religious experience of the human race. In the last ten years of his life, Wach was often mistakenly thought to be in the camp of the second approach to comparative religion at Chicago, which necessitated his stating repeatedly that while the philosophy of religion applies an abstract philosophical idea of what religion is to the data of empirical, historical studies, the history of religions begins with the investigation of religious phenomena, from which, it is hoped, a pattern of "meaning" will emerge. The history of religions' inquiry into the "meaning" of religious phenomena *leads* one to questions of a philosophical and metaphysical nature, but the history of religions as such cannot deal with those questions philosophically.

Wach believed that the history of religions was a discipline to be taught in a university, ideally simultaneously in a department of theology and in the humanities. He himself taught primarily in the Divinity School but he had an intellectual outlet in the Committee on the History of Culture. He devoted much time as well to the social sciences, participating, for example, in an interdisciplinary seminar called "The Birth of Civilization" under the direction of the great anthropologist Robert Redfield. But basically he was happiest when surrounded by his own students, the so-called Sangha. He was convinced, in fact, that each of his students would be an important emissary for the history of religions.

In retrospect, I wonder how happy Wach was in Chicago. He lived in the twentieth century, but he was more at home with the nineteenth, academically speaking. Cosmopolitan though he was, he had, after all, been driven out of Germany, and his intellectual gaze never wandered very far from Dilthey's *Erlebnis* (experience), *Ausdruck* (expression), and *Verstehen* (understanding). Be that as it may, Wach remained quite sure about the nature of his calling. As he once stated:

> The need for *understanding*, understanding people and peoples, their thought and affections, their words and deeds, has impressed the author from his youth. He chose the problem of hermeneutics—the theory of interpretation—as the subject of an extensive historical study [meaning *Das Verstehen*, 3 vols.]. He has tried to carry out his work both as a scholar and as a teacher, in two continents, with a view to practicing and teaching understanding. Two wars brought home to him even more clearly the urgency of helping to create the conditions for understanding among nations.[8]

Wach was delighted to deliver the Barrows Lectures on Comparative Religion in India in 1952 and the American Council of Learned Societies Lectures in the History of Religions in 1954–55.[9] In late spring 1955, he attended the Congress of the International Association for the History of Religions (IAHR) in Rome. His later travels confirmed for him a statement made early in his Chicago days: "The European centers of learning, nearly all of which were affected by war, continue to devote great interest to the study of Eastern civilizations and religions. But the handicap under which they have to work places an increased responsibility upon American scholarship and initiative."[10] And, true to his own words, Wach was determined to do his share of teaching and scholarship in America. Just before his death in August 1955, he received the coveted invitation from Marburg University offering him the chair once occupied by his mentor, Rudolf Otto. Tempting though this offer was, especially since he felt the kind hand of his former teacher, Friedrich Heiler, in the invitation, Wach declined the offer because "my vocation is to develop what I have started at Chicago."[11]

This volume contains representative essays from each of the major phases of Wach's scholarly career. From the first phase we have chosen two essays. The first, "Master and Disciple," was originally published as *Meister und Jünger: Zwei religions-soziologische Betrachtungen* (Tübingen: J. C. B. Mohr, 1925). The English translation by Susanne Heigl-Wach and Frederick Streng first appeared in the *Journal of Religion* 42, no. 1 (January 1962), 1–21. The second, "Mahāyāna Buddhism," was originally published as *Mahayana, besonders im Hinblick auf das Saddharma-Pundarika-Sutra* (Munich-Neubiberg: Schloss, Untersuchungen 16, 1925). The English translation by Nancy Auer Falk has not appeared before. Also included are two essays from Wach's second phase: "Wilhelm von Humboldt" (which was found in Wach's desk after his death) and "Sociology of Religion," written at Brown University and published first in George Gurvitch and Wilbert E. Moore, eds., *Twentieth Century Sociology* (New York: Philosophical Library, 1945). Four essays represent Wach's third and last phase: "Radhakrishnan and the Comparative Study of Religion," which appeared in P. A. Schilpp, ed., *The Philosophy of Sarvepalli Radhakrishnan* (New York: Tudor Publishing Co., 1952), pp. 443–58; "Religion in America," which was based on notes from lectures given at various universities in the United States; "On Teaching History of Religions," which appeared in a memorial volume to honor G. van der Leeuw called *Pro Regno Pro Sanctuario* (Nijkerk: G. F. Callenbach, 1950), pp. 525–32; and "On Understanding," which appeared in A. A. Roback, ed., *The Albert Schweitzer Jubilee Book* (Cambridge, Mass.: SCI-Art Publishers, 1946), pp. 131–46. All are reproduced here with proper permission. These selections will, we hope, provide readers with some understanding of Wach's intellectual pilgrimage.

Joachim Wach's spirit lives among his former students, to whom this volume is dedicated. I wish to take this opportunity to thank Charles E. Smith, Paul Bernabeo, and Elly Dickason of Macmillan Publishing Company for their advice and assistance in bringing together this collection.

Thanks also are due to Dean Franklin I. Gamwell of the Divinity School of the University of Chicago; to my secretary, Martha Morrow-Vojacek, and to Peter Chemery, my present research assistant, upon whose extensive care and attention my recent work has depended.

Lastly I wish to express my special appreciation to Professor Gregory Alles of Western Maryland College, co-editor of this volume and of this book's companion volume (also published by Macmillan this year), entitled *Introduction to the History of Religions,* consisting of Wach's 1924 habilitation thesis, *Religionswissenschaft* and six articles which appeared in *Religion in Geschichte und Gegenwart* (1930). In both Professor Alles has cheerfully carried a heavy burden because of my poor health.

MASTER AND DISCIPLE: TWO RELIGIO-SOCIOLOGICAL STUDIES

Only there man's nature is sustained where the darksome offering is retained.

Der Stern des Bundes

The disciple is not above his master.

Matt. 10:24

The Master and Disciple—The Teacher and Student

The disciple is always associated with a master, the student with a teacher. Let us speak of an ideal teacher-student relationship based solely on subject matter and not on the personalities of the teacher and student. The bond is constituted through common interest in the object of study; the student respects the teacher as the possessor and mediator of certain crafts, a body of knowledge or an accomplished skill; he considers him worthy when this treasure is great and significant and when the teacher is willing to give of it freely.

It is not the person who is admired and esteemed, but a certain faculty, a skill, knowledge, or capability. The human prestige is entirely dependent upon the inherent relevance and respect, the importance and value of the object of study. The student admires in the teacher the greatness and significance of his learning; and his merit consists in his willingness to give freely of this treasure. The student is dear to the

1

teacher to the extent that he is willing to open himself to the
teacher's communication; the student's value depends on his
individual success or failure to appropriate the subject matter.
This entire relationship is born and lives by means of the
common interest in the object of study. A diversion from it
results in the disintegration of the relationship between them.
From this we can understand the replaceability of the person;
any given teacher like any given student is replaceable; if he
is not, it is merely that none can actually be found to take
his place.

The relationship of the master to the disciple is found
where the tie is personal—not based primarily on subject
matter; the individuality of the master and the disciple con-
sequently gains central significance. The master does not enjoy
this esteem because he conveys something useful, something
transferable from his possession to the disciple; it is not the
result of the fortunate possession of a particular artistic skill.
Rather, the significance for the disciple rests in the master's
personality, whose very character and activity are individual
and irreplaceable. Corresponding to this the choice of the
disciple is grounded in the master's inclination, which grows
out of a deep conviction regarding his "calling" to discipleship.
The favorite disciple is not he who advances or shows promise
of advancement toward mastering the common subject matter
(which may also be there but is not decisive in this relationship);
he is the one with whom the master cultivates a profound
personal relationship. The disciple understands the master;
the student understands the teaching—the skill of the teacher.
A student makes himself what he is by his own individual
effort. A disciple is chosen; he is called to understand the
master. The disciple must be touched to the core by his
personality. The beloved master must be an essential part of
his own existence.

The teacher and student, united through a bond of work
on a common task, form a series of links in which the student
in his own proper time will also become a teacher. Conversely,
the master and disciple in themselves represent the beginning
and the end, a cosmos in itself; the disciple will never become

a master. Accordingly, the teacher heads a school; the master forms a circle around himself. The teacher gives of himself to the student without receiving anything in return; personal relationship means nothing to the teacher, but the master-disciple relationship at its very core is one of mutual significance. The master becomes a master only in relationship to a disciple. Here we are not emphasizing a merely verbal correlation but rather a profound fact: that the master only becomes fully aware of the sense of his mastership in its highest and final form through a perceptive and comprehending disciple, and it is the disciple who ordains his master to mastership. The master reads his calling in the eye of his disciple, just as the disciple hears destiny speak in and through the master.

The teacher gives of his knowledge, of his ability; the master gives himself. What the master is to the disciple, he is through his existence, that is, if he is to be master, he must be himself. What he is, he had achieved through his own development; and what he has become through this development is always actually present in its totality. Therefore, what he has to say is always existentially significant; it must be understood from the standpoint of existence, for it pertains to the total man. The disciple understands the master only when he understands him in the context of existence. Fundamentally this means that the master must renounce all hope of being fully understood, because to understand him fully would mean to become the master, to know the great mystery of renunciation, to know that the highest fulfilment is possible only in another person. This is the melancholy awareness of all masters—that no heirs are provided for the master, that the sweetest and best fruit which ripens for him never can be given away, because whoever comes to himself indeed comes only to himself. This characterizes the attitude of the master: a touch of gentle resignation, of understanding kindness, and of silent grief.

The most sacred moment in the relation of the master to his disciple comes when the master finally turns the disciple back to himself; it reveals the significance of the master for his disciple; it is the moment in which the relationship is most intimate. Yet, at the same time, it is that moment in which the master appears most remote: above the relationship of master and disciple is written the word "farewell." It is the specific tragedy of the master's life that he is destined to direct everything toward this parting. Instead of completely drawing to himself, he must completely thrust away; instead of moving from distance to the intimate unity, he must move in the opposite direction.

Therefore the master can only love his disciple with a tinge of sadness. The disciple does not understand the master, though the master means everything to him; he loses himself in the greatness of the master and seeks to comprehend him existentially. His highest goal is to be most intimately related to this master. So "he follows after him," until the hour of decision comes, which always must be the hour of parting; then the disciple despairs either of the master or of himself. He must choose either himself and take leave of the master, who was dearer to him than all things, or he must deny himself, continuing to love the master, and so destroy completely the master's labor. The master will love this disciple because of this devotion, but the disciple who left him will not be forgotten by him. This is the double recognition which is earned by the master's character. On the one hand, his sacrifice, even though not understood, is still effective and bears fruit, for what has proceeded out of the existence procreates and remains living in existence; and, on the other, the consequences of love remain even into solitude, reverence, and faithful service, enjoying the severity of the task. Therefore, when the evening of life comes for the master, and the friends of his best years go their ways, the disciple remains with him. The disciple performs the service of love for him, not because he knows what really constitutes the mystery of the final loneliness which no love shares and no undertanding can brighten, but because he has fully realized that his place is here.

The teacher survives in his work; the master survives in those who have experienced his influence and bear witness to him. All others can only surmise it. The disciple testifies to what the master was to him when he speaks of his master: as he has seen the master, so he paints his picture that it might be imprinted on the memory. He alone possesses the full value of the image, and others are dependent on him for their view of the master. And as he, in order to make known the beloved figure, tries to transmit the features of the master's character to others, so also the other disciples do it, in fact all who surround the master. In them burns the desire to share what they have known by firsthand experience, and they are eager to tell others. But the secret of the master is really the influence of his personality; and only he who has experienced it can evaluate it. So from the beginning the labor of the disciple carries the germ of the tragic necessity that it must fail. Whoever saw the master cannot communicate the experience which he alone had; any talk of it is bound to fail. Each story concerning the master is a legend which has its own action and time. The legend itself changes when it is once established along more universal lines and has received a form that is easily apprehended; as such it reaches those who come after, for whom it becomes tradition and history. But what passes between men in life must be experienced directly.

The teacher knows that his work remains; the master lives in the knowledge that nothing of what he gives can remain. The teacher gives a definite subject matter; the master provides only stimulus. In the disposition of the master, the significance of the moment is important; as for his attitude, the whole problem of time is of prime importance. From the recognition of transitoriness and of change comes the understanding of the need for the right moment. "Kairos" is the key term here: therefore no eternity can bring back what was missed before; only the sacred hour begets the sacred knowledge; therefore many hours must be nourished from this one. The teacher carefully measures his time and dedicates as much as he is able to the task of teaching—worry for fear that his task will not be accomplished would never occur to him, since he knows that after him his students will become teachers in turn, and so he will live on. But the master would never worry about his time or his own security in any sense. Now and then, at ease, he gives all he has. All the sweetness of the moment, with its immediate demands, its unending horizon, the weight of a thousand possibilities, the apprehension of death and perishability, loosens the heart and tongue; and it is as though nothing had been before, and as though nothing will ever be again. It can happen only once; it is unique. And as only one being can produce *this one* thing in this one particular moment, so it is possible to produce it only in one person, in the disciple who is awake in the decisive hour. Then both the world and all time around them are swallowed up; through the transitory human frailty shines the eternal, before which all humanity and human accomplishments are futile. A faint notion of the divine is dawning, which never is revealed to mere effort, not even the most persistent.

This means that the master's life is filled with activity and unrest, while that of the teacher moves along in serene security. This is indeed the distress and mystery of this disposition, the fact that it can never be permitted "to forget itself"—neither in surrender nor in service, so that it is continually giving of itself. Whenever it gives, it gives out of a depth in which living powers are always operative and in which there is always life, which means that there is continual conflict. The teacher is consumed by his task, his work; the master consumes himself. "And as you consume yourself, you are full of light." The teacher has the truth which he wants to promulgate—or else he is on the way to finding it; but the master has nothing which he can give to all.

The teacher meets the student in the area of the subject matter: he teaches him to cultivate the soil, and they work on the ground together. Or the student sits at the feet of the teacher, who speaks to him from his lofty height. The master would raise his disciple up to himself; he would raise him higher, even above himself: they never meet on the same plane. The teacher and student have something in common on which they work together and which unites them. The master and his disciple are either completely united or not at all, and they live with each other in this relationship day in and day out. The teacher praises the swift foot, the skilled hand, the sharp eye, and the keen intellect of the student; while in the master's eye there are no such distinctions. For him, body and soul remain undivided. A standard and a measure are held up to the disciple: to exist, which means to live from a central norm; and this norm is the very living body of the disciple. Such is the meaning of the master's requirement, that the body also love beauty.

To be the typical student and to belong to the same school as one's teacher is a unifying experience. The point of contact which expresses the common bond between teacher and student also provides the foundation upon which the school is established. In this joint enterprise everything that is primarily objective is in the foreground, and where subjectivity plays a part, it is only accidentally interwoven in this relation between person and thing. Everything individual—all personal effort and striving—recedes to the background and is of no validity or interest.

Discipleship is different: being one of a group of disciples under a master is no basis for mutual love; rather it is often the basis for hate. From the beginning it seems impossible that someone else should have a part in the relationship that ties the disciple to his master (it is a condition which has its foundation in the incomparability and uniqueness of individuality), so, in principle, no way leads from one of them to another. Convinced that he is devoted to and open to the master as no other is, the disciple feels a passionate conviction to claim his master's love in preference to all else and all others. Thus, the human, the all-too-human emotions of envy and jealousy arise. Of course such emotions are also known among students, but they are not intrinsic to scholarly activity. The sinister act of the disciple, who from jealousy betrays the master, is the most shattering expression of this impulse, and it is conceivable only in such a relationship.

Let us compare now discipleship with the school when each is deprived of its head: here the situation is nearly reversed. Within the school, embittered disputes are raised concerning the "authentic interpretation" of the legacy left by the teacher; a contest concerning a successor sets in; the fellow student who becomes the opponent will be fought more desperately than the most wicked enemy. But this is not so among the disciples who are deprived of their master. In the true spirit of their master those who are left behind—who often possess entirely different individualities—are brought together through the image which is sacred to each of them. Moreover, the personal distress, common loneliness, and concern over the future produce a great unity. The work of the master will not continue, since no one can continue it except he who began it. And where it appears as though this did occur, a new master has arisen or a school has been assembled about a teacher.

The name of a powerful teacher is associated with his work, and in it his reputation is secured. The personality of the master lives on as an effective force. Of both, however, the word of Daniel has been spoken: They shall shine as the splendor of the heavens.

On the Meaning of the Master's Life

This essay is about the master and disciple. Our concern is not with the specific content of the teachings proclaimed by the exalted masters. Rather, the following discourse will deal with the meaning and value of the master's life, the "existence" of the master.

First let us consider the tradition of Buddhism regarding its master. We are told that one night, in the forest of Urvela, Gotama—while he was lost in solitary meditation, going through continually higher states of ecstatic self-renunciation—attained release and revelation of this release. In this sacred moment he grasped the knowledge about the suffering of the world, the sources of suffering, its annihilation and the way to its annihilation. The night in which the Buddha attained this knowledge—as he was seated under the tree—is the holy night of the Buddhist world; in this night Gotama became the Buddha. The creatures of all the worlds were elated; gods and men shouted with joy. As the saving wisdom in the blessed

munity itself, is certainly important; yet the justification regarding our essential distinction can hardly be doubted. The consideration of the particular kind of *charisma*—upon which Max Weber has placed special emphasis in his religious-sociological treatise—is not decisive for us. We proceed from the experience of the respective personality; we will not only analyze it psychologically but understand it in its full intention by showing its meaning for the master's whole existence and the consequences of the master's life.

Instead of recognizing the meaning and role of each person in light of his effectiveness in providing a metaphysical value, let us consider the crucial element to lie in the consciousness in itself. It is the peculiar driving force in the master's existence—the ground out of which his whole attitude toward the world, his whole thought and activity, must be understood.

The knowledge which "the called-one" receives is a tragic one. Its content is tragic; the nature of the world and his own being are felt to be full of sorrow. But this knowledge can also be called tragic in its effect on the existence itself of the master. Because this knowledge is tragic, the struggle in which the calling becomes evident is so hard; in it the thought of sacrifice is affirmed for the first time. The chosen one knows that he struggles, discerns, suffers, and succeeds by renouncing himself; he struggles, suffers, and succeeds for others. As it was stated by the poet: The fruit of the tree is not for the tree. Therefore, as expressed in the words of the Buddhist teachings, the last great temptation is to remain a savior for one's self, a *pratyeka-buddha*, and to reject the terrifying call of the *samyaksaṃbuddha*—to become a redeemer for all. A grandiose thought! In the midst of a suffering, fighting, turbulent world caught in tumultuous struggle, there is this one man who grasps the great thought of peace and knows about redemption in the midst of the chaos of meaninglessness and despair—one man who has found a meaning. This is the picture which the buddhist legends portray for us. The Buddha, surrounded by the fury of the elements and hosts of assaulting demons and spirits, is sunk in deep comtemplation while beholding the secrets of the holy truth.

To have this insight means loneliness. The beatitude of this tremendous knowledge is balanced by a dreadful, exalted, echoless silence. Four times seven days the Buddha continued to delight in the perception which he had gained. Again and again the sermons, which are handed down to us in the holy texts, make reference to this loneliness.

Knowledge creates loneliness and abandonment; but this does not incite the decision to share it. The chosen one feels sorry for the erring and searching men whom he henceforth sees in the light of the full perception. The desire to be a deliverer moves him: he would bring peace to them, for which they yearn; he would teach them. Will they be able to comprehend what he has to say to them? "It is difficult, mysterious, deep, hidden from the crude senses," thought the Buddha. We understand the struggle in which the impulses contend with each other: to remain silent or to speak out. But the thought of sacrifice is so intimately merged with the very nature of the master's existence, it hardly seems possible that the decisive "Yes" could not emerge, sealing the master's sacrificial path.

When Jesus knew himself as the Messiah, he knew the necessity of his own sacrificial suffering. We do not know the exact point in his life in which this consciousness came upon him, unless we would accept the baptism in the Jordan—where, according to Scripture, the Spirit of God came upon him—as the breakthrough of this consciousness. From the earliest beginning of his public appearance he is conscious of his particular mission; from the first his words and work are overshadowed by the destiny which he took upon himself in an unknown hour, by the knowledge which preceded this resolve to sacrifice. To this hour, as also to that other mysterious ὥρα (hour), point all those profound words—for example, concerning the ransom money in Matthew; and the words of deep suffering found in John: "I give up my life for the sheep," and "No one takes it from me, but I give it up by myself." Up to the climax in which he realized a single-mindedness with his destiny—as it is expressed in the so-called High-priestly Prayer (John, chap. 17)—is a high resolve whose confirmation is the fulfilment: "It is finished." But between those two moments, the unknown first and this last, temptations continually seized the Chosen One. We know about it from the story of the temptation according to Matthew and Luke; we learn of it in that short, most clearly delivered story of Matthew about Peter's request: "Lord, preserve yourself. . . ." (This is the memorable situation corresponding to the conversation of Buddha with Ananda near Vesali.) But above all it is in the shattering account of the struggle in Gethsemane and the confirmation in the Letter to the Hebrews. The cognition of the nature of the world and of the metaphysical significance of one's own self in it; the knowledge about the mission; the "Yes" to destiny; the sacrificial thought; and the last struggle and hesitation are clearly portrayed in that passage from Luke's Gospel: "I am come to cast a fire upon the earth; would that it were already kindled. I have a baptism to be baptized with; and how I am constrained until it is accomplished!"

Let us consider antiquity: Did not the Greeks know about Chiron, the wise centaur, who instructed Achilles in playing the lyre; who introduced the mortal son of the immortal gods to the knowledge of the mysteries, guiding him out of the darkness of the Dionysian natural existence into the Apollonian kingdom of light; who showed him the way of transitoriness to immortal existence, himself a delivered deliverer? Before us stands Empedocles, the old philosopher of Agrigentum, who has ever and again found admiring disciples up to the present time: the prophetic thinker and seer, the leader of those pious ones, whose heart longs for the redemption—whom Hoelderlin, a man very close to the Greeks, has given to us anew. In this magnificent poem everything that is decisive for the existence of a master becomes clear to us: the knowledge about the suffering of the world, the recognition of the calling, the "Yes" to it, the "Yes" to destiny, the thought of sacrifice, the temptation, the anxiety and hesitation before the final decision. Indeed, here it is expressed in the ancient Greek idiom:

Divine nature is manifested

Divinely only through Man; thus again
The race which attempts so much recognizes it.
Yet when the mortal, whose heart divine nature
Filled with its delight, has announced it,
Oh, let it break that vessel in pieces
Lest it serve to other uses
And divine things become human works.

There is no more profound expression of the master-disciple relationship than that given by Hoelderlin in the relation of Empedocles-Pausanias. Hardly anywhere is the tragic aspect in the master's existence brought to a more moving expression. Or let us consider Socrates, who, according to Nietzsche, is an ambiguous figure in antiquity. Is not also Socrates a "master" in the sense we are attempting to develop? Something of the exalted sorrow is spread over his being and works, which comes from the knowledge of the metaphysical condition of the world, the calling and the end. The later thinker Søren Kierkegaard, who probably most profoundly understood him, spoke once of the midwifery "of Socrates as the highest relationship between men." "Because," according to him, "between man and man μαιεύεσθαι [midwifery] is the highest, the γεννᾶν [engendering] belongs to God." This throws a light on the inner existence of Socrates; one side of the master's life is profoundly characterized: the resignation in the highest sense, the sacrificial thought. Certainly Socrates specifically rejects thereby all claim to a metaphysical significance of his person; but is he not Greek? He is not only teacher, mediator of knowledge and capability, adviser, leader in ethical and political concerns, but, as his death shows—which must be interpreted as the emerging of the master's sacrifice—he is also a master in the highest sense of the word. In this way Plato had also understood him.

The melancholy and gentle sadness which characterize the life of the master show his readiness for sacrifice; it appears even in the serenity of fulfilment, as in the ancient piety of Empedocles, toward destiny. It shines through the irony of Socrates. It forms the dark-gold background against which the radiant words of Jesus are set off. It is the "Yes" to destiny—

the once-spoken; yet, ever again in the master's life it must be repeated, until the end, until the fulfilment. It is this "Yes" which is ever present and which surrounds every deed and word of the master with a touch of deep sorrow. Thus we learn that the master also is bound; the task which he undertakes acquires ultimate dimensions from God, from destiny. The whole existence of the master signifies a growing-up to this call; through his entire existence the argument with the highest authority continues; the hour of the call is only its most intense concentration.

This "Yes" implies the renunciation of the splendor and happiness of the world, of home and of love, of all ties and associations; to offer one's self for sacrifice is, in a higher sense, necessary; to participate in the coherent development of events as destiny has determined. This renunciation is expressed most comprehensively by the Buddha. Ever and again in the Holy Scriptures we meet the explicit abandonment of all earthly happiness, symbolized in the story of Prince Gotama's encounters with, and his flight from, the world. At first sight this seems to be no painful resignation, since everything from which the Enlightened One turns away is indeed empty, vain, and idle. Here psychological interpretation must go deeper, for it is precisely this which is the difficulty of the knowledge to which the chosen one is called: that before its gaze all the glitter and glory of the world became nothing. The Chosen One sees that mankind lives cheerfully and painlessly; the old world sprouts and blooms continually ever anew; life goes on, in the ups and downs of its natural rhythm. But he also knows that all this is not the "true," not the decisive; it is not that upon which all depends. In the hour of his calling he experiences the mystery that from now on raises his existence to the tragic level, which makes it lonely. From the time this knowledge is awakened in him, he is excluded from this eternal play, from the cheerful thoughtless pleasures of everyday life, from ordinary happiness. It is very profound that the tradition had the Buddha grow up in worldly splendor and earthly delights; he must know them before they become shallow to him.

Profound and beautiful also is the late story, which we have previously mentioned, concerning the temptation at Vesali. Here life itself seduced the aged man; the beauty of the world threatened to draw him into its spell. But the world can be no enduring place for him. The master's existence is one of loneliness. "The foxes have holes, and the birds of the air have nests, but the Son of Man has nowhere to lay his head." He does not know the intimate fellowship in which the members of the family circle gather; he is homeless also in this sense. To become a disciple of Buddha means to renounce everything: parents and kindred, wife and child, house and home. Jesus said to the disciples: Whoever leaves his house, or brothers and sisters, or father or mother, or wife or child for my name will receive a hundred fold and inherit eternal life. It sounds even harsher in Luke: Anyone who follows me and does not hate his father, mother, wife, child, brothers, sisters, and also his own life—he cannot be my disciple. And from the same we read: Whoever does not renounce all that he has cannot be my disciple.

Even the love of women cannot bind the chosen one. Neither condemnation nor contempt of a woman and marriage is thereby expressed—although such features are found—but it is the renunciation in favor of the noble task resulting from the knowledge of the reality of things. Once Ananda asked the Buddha—who himself left behind a wife and a small son in order to reach his aim, and who according to Udana explicitly praised Sangamaji when he had deserted his wife and child—"How should we, Lord, behave in regard to a woman?"—"You should avoid seeing them." Ananda: "If we, however, do see them, Lord, what should we do then?"—"Do not speak with them." Ananda: "If we must, however, speak with them, Lord, what then?" "Then you must be watchful of yourself." The master himself had rejected all passion of worldly love when the daughters of Mara tried to seduce him.

One cannot fail to recognize that those passages in the holy texts, which unwittingly and without intent touch this relationship, keep the woman disciple both inwardly and outwardly at a certain distance from the master. None of the women disciples, as the texts tell us, is near to the dying master. The Divyavadana tells us a temptation story of Ananda, who is blamed because—as the Cullavagga reports—he permitted women at the corpse of Buddha, who by their sorrow defiled the corpse. "O Criton, let someone take this woman home," said Socrates, as Xantippe appeared in the prison to take her final leave of him. Empedocles, according to the magnificent poem, also removed himself from his female disciples before he entered his final course; nothing is left to them but the mourning of his departure and the realization of their loss.

We know from the Gospels the appreciation that Jesus had for the womanly disposition. There are many episodes reported, especially in John, concerning his relationship with women, which a later time changed to the ascetic. This later tendency is found in the well-known expression, attributed to John by the so-called "Apostolic Church Regulation":

> When the master prayed over the bread and the cup, and blessed them with the words: This is my body and blood, he did not permit the women to stay with us (Martha said, on account of Mary, because he saw her smiling. Mary said: I laughed no more). And he said this to us before, when he taught: The weak are saved through the strong.

Next to him, Peter, above all, is portrayed in a later time as having particular hostility toward women. "I am afraid of Peter," expressed Mary in the gnostic writing Pistis Sophia, "because he threatens men and hates our sex." But we do not have to reduce ourselves to the apocryphal writings of the New Testament to observe the basic thrust of this one-sided emphasis. As the master was without a home, so he never fell in love with a woman. This the Church Fathers knew: Justin, of course Tertullian (who emphasized this to its fullest), Clement, and Origen. Ἡ ἰσχὺς τῶν ἐγκρατευομένων, ὁ στέφανος τῶν παρθένων, ἡ σωφροσύνη τῶν μονογάμων.[2] So Jesus is called.

We have seen already that a later period portrays him as recommending this asceticism to others. Thus, to the Record of John, the Lord himself through his appearance prevented John, who was in the process of entering matrimony, from getting married—one story which is parallel to the account of Ananda's temptation and the intervention of Buddha. The mysterious saying in Matt. 19:12 may have given a point of reference permitting such an interpretation. From the Gospel of the gnostic Marcion we learn that the Jews in their court proceedings rebuked Jesus because he broke up marriage and destroyed the bonds of family life. "The ascetic Gotama," said the people, "has come to bring childless times, widowhood, and ruin of the racial stock."

All this cannot surprise us. The master rejects even this earthly bond for himself. Through his call to knowledge, he steps out of the ever continuing cycle of reproduction in which nature knows itself as being eternal in its creatures. In nature all things call to one another—as Schopenhauer says: Today as yesterday, we are always all together.

The renunciation is joined at bottom with the mission. It is not important whether and how far the master systematizes it and makes it a requirement; it is imminent in the master's existence. From this perspective it is also proved once more that loneliness is essential to this existence.

No one can share this loneliness with him; even the disciples cannot. For an instant—as we saw—the temptation to hold back his knowledge, to side-step the difficult path together with all misunderstanding and disappointment, overcomes the master. Nothing like this is reported to us concerning Jesus. But is it false to suppose that he, who in the final hour prayed: "Lord, if it is possible, let this cup pass from me," also knew the desire to be freed from this path of sacrifice—he who continually experienced with deepest grief how little those closest to him understood? Nevertheless the master knows that everything—all his suffering, his agony—is in vain and that his sacrifice is futile unless he succeeds in planting the truth in one soul that has opened itself to him.

In the cases of Jesus and Buddha, the election of the disciples followed immediately after the decisive experience of the call. Buddha enlisted his first disciples in Benares; they were the five pious devotees who before his enlightenment had practiced asceticism with him. "In that time there were six holy men in the world, Buddha himself and the five disciples." Jesus went out and called those whom he wanted to draw unto himself: "Follow me!" It has been justifiably emphasized[3] that by using this means of selection, Jesus promoted a principle of selection in which the choice was not based on personal worth but in which a fellowship of destiny predominated. He did not choose the most distinguished, the best, the most able; he chose those to whom his heart turned out of a deep sense of inner affinity. Despite the character of the fellowship which developed around the master, there existed a definite relationship between the master and each of the disciples which was determined by the individual nature and personality of the disciple. The image which one disciple forms of the master is necessarily different from the image formed by any other; it is colored through his "relative a priori"—regarding individuality, temperament, and disposition. On the other hand, seen from the point of view of the master, the disciples constitute a unity. There are, no doubt, types of disciples: a type of Jesus-disciple, of Buddha-disciple, and there is a type of Hellenic, or Sufist, discipleship.

The disciples have a threefold significance for the master. They are first of all the "representatives of mankind"—ignorant mankind. In spite of all initiation and all association with the master, they remain in need of instruction to the end: they can never understand the master, never basically comprehend the idea of sacrifice. In part they belong to the master; in part to "the world"; and therefore a cleavage continues to exist between the master and themselves which makes the master lonely. He knows about it, but he is glad that those whom he loves are spared from the gravity and burden of the knowledge which is laid upon him. Therefore he blesses them; but in difficult hours of temptation he suffers.

Second, the disciples are the master's companions. Insofar as they are capable, they are near to him. They share his outward existence and try to make it easy. They are always in readiness, and in some particularly high and choice hours we find them in closest association with the master. Then he discloses part of his being and his knowledge to them—as much as is possible for them to grasp. Out of this human need for men who are near him, the Jesus of the Acts of John says to the disciples: "I need you, come to me"—a word which almost sounds blasphemous to a person who sees only the representative character of the disciples.

Third, the disciples are the apostles of the master; they are the proclaimers of his "teaching." As such they do not interest us here, because this essay deals with the relation of the master and disciple primarily in regard to the master's existence.

The varied significance of the disciples is clearly distinguished in the historical individuality of each of Jesus' disciples—as we learn to know them from the canonical and aprocryphal writings of the New Testament. Nowhere do we find the "representative" aspect of the disciple stronger, deeper, and more impressive than in the figure of Peter. We shall recall only two of those unforgettable episodes between the Lord and the follower disciple which illustrate what we have been saying: the rescue of the sinking Peter (Matthew, chap. 14) and Peter's betrayal (Luke, chap. 22). John the Evangelist appears in the incarnation of the conception of the companion, the disciple friend. We know from Scripture that the Lord loved him: "John," the Lord says to him according to the Acts of John (chap. 98), "there is one who must hear this from me, because I need one who should hear it."

Once more let us turn back to the figures of antiquity. Certainly in regard to the crucial elements there is a similarity in the significance of the disciples for the master. It appears clearly in the touching and beautiful characterization of Pausanias, whom Hoelderlin has depicted as a companion to Empedocles: the only person who is close to the master, to whom the master inclines himself lovingly and trustingly, and yet whom he must so often instruct and correct, who cannot understand the highest and final thing—the necessity and the loneliness of the sacrifice. Yet he calls him "Son! Son of my soul"—the only human being he loves. It appears in Socrates, from whose circle of disciples so many a character and name are known to us. And like Socrates, also in Zarathustra—as has been shown to us again recently in a profound manner—and in whom the last of our great thinkers [Nietzsche] envisioned for himself the "ideal master."

Concerning the *sravakas,* the circle of disciples which assembled about the Buddha, it is said that there were only types, not individuals—as in the following account:

> Each of the great disciples is just like another so that each is hard to distinguish from the other; each is a model of highest purity, highest inner peace, highest devotion to Buddha.

The representatives of the suffering and erring world are the ones whom the enlightened one instructs ever and again.

Some of them, however, come to life for us: Condanna, the confessor; Sariputta, one of the disciples who is allowed to hear a word similar to that spoken by the Lord to Peter: he compares him to the eldest son of a world ruler, who, following the king, together with him sets in motion the wheel of rulership which this king lets roll over the earth; his friend Maha-Moggallana, the possessor of mysterious miraculous power, whose beautiful account of being called is passed on to us in the Mahavagga. Further, there is Kassapa, the former barber of Upali, a true apostle; Rahula, the Buddha's son; Devadatta, the Judas Iscariot of Buddhism; and Ananda Upatthaka, a friend and companion of the exalted one as no other, of whose temptation and confirmation the texts tell us, as in the great sutra concerning the end of the master.

A later period put the most varied teachings and sayings into the mouths of these disciples. Ever and again the well-known figures appeared and preached their sermons to the honor of the master or for the conversion of the ignorant and wavering. As in a chorus, their voices are heard in the Theragata, the "Monks' Hymns." The disciples' words which are handed down to us in the Sutta-Nipata sound like a common confession:

> To him my spirit looks, as if my eyes could see him
> By night by day, fixed without fatigue.

Reverently dedicated to him, I wait for the morning.
From him, I feel, I cannot be separated.

There has been far too little interest in the disciples of
Jesus. At all times the most earnest, the most impressive, and
the most fruitful concern for them has been shown by artists.
These—especially the German masters of the high Middle
Ages, but also the later Italians—have understood the wonderful fascination of those figures, who, coming out of and
disappearing into the dark, surround and accompany the figure
of the Redeemer. The disciples remain halfway between individuals of flesh and blood and impressive, carefully stylized
types. In the first century after the coming of the Lord there
was a strong interest in those who had surrounded him during
his lifetime, and a rich and interesting literature testified to
it. Thus we follow Peter and participate in his struggle with
Simon, the magician; we hear of the tragic fate of his daughter
and experience his cruel crucifixion. We follow John, the
eternally pure apostle of Asia, in his wondrous deeds; we get
to know the extraordinary illumination which he received,
and we see his joyful end. We accompany Bartholomew in his
struggle against the Indian idols; we see James the son of
Zebedee contending with a sorcerer and converting the Span-
iards, and James the son of Alphaeus, the courageous and
upright witness, hurled down from the pinnacle of the temple,
praying for his enemies in the words of his Lord. We see
Matthew suffer the most terrifying tortures for his Lord's sake.
We are led into the dangerous and difficult situation into
which Andrew brought himself by his strict asceticism; we
experience the terrible martyrdom of Philip, the apostle to
Asia Minor; and we travel with the apostle Thomas way over
to India in order to learn of his wonderful experiences and
deeds. We follow Simon the Zealot to Babylonia and Persia—
Simon, who already as a boy was permitted to hear the promise
of the future master. Thus many things are communicated to
us concerning life of the master and his intimate relationship
with his disciples.

We learn much that is believable and unbelievable—the
repulsive and the attractive. Who could not but be grasped

by the descriptions which the Acts of John—the most beautiful and profound of those mysterious writings—gives to us of the last gathering of the Lord with his disciples, culminating in the account of the magnificent hymn which those intone who are united in the ecstatic cult dance. The writings of the heretical groups, particularly, know how to tell the most miraculous things. The disciples enjoy high, indeed extraordinary, esteem in these circles; they are given a kind of metaphysical meaning as it is already indicated in that passage which the Ephraim Commentary passes on to us: "I have chosen you before the existence of the world"; and this esteem is expressed in the gnostic Pistis Sophia in the most elaborate manner. All this is late stylization as it is active in the developing legends of the masters.

More beautiful and true than those superhuman exaggerated miracle workers and saints are the infinitely more lifelike figures of the disciples in the Gospels. In the former we find a parallel to the description of the disciples as seen in the Mahayana Sutras (I mention only the *Saddharma-Pundarika,* the Lotus of Good Religion). A later apology, which did not understand the importance of simplicity, believed that it must excuse its humanity. Compared to the simple account of Luke, how clumsy and inwardly untrue rings the report of the Acts of Peter, seeking to interpret the denial by Peter, explaining that "godless dogs" had duped him and lured him into a trap. The idea of "disciple" demands that the pure "human-ness" be expressed. The Lord himself, according to the Acts of Peter, said in regard to the disciples: *"qui mecum sunt, non me intellexerunt."*4 We understand the deep necessity of this incomprehensibility (cf. also Luke 9:49 and 50). It is very possible that occasionally sorrow and bitterness came upon the master when he called to mind the human, all-too-human, nature of those about him; but he knew that it could not be otherwise—and therefore was good. "I have yet many things to say to you," says the Christ of St. John, "but you cannot hear them now."

With an understanding gaze of love the master embraced these men who were permitted to share one destiny with him.

He blessed their purely human nature; but in the pangs of his loneliness when thinking of the sacrifice, he felt their distance from him; he longed for their sympathy—which he could not have. There is no deeper, no more moving, illustration of this situation than the story of the struggle in Gethsemane as Matthew has given it to us. The master asks them: "Could you not watch with me one hour?" And then it reads: "and again he came and found them sleeping, for their eyes were heavy. And he left them and went away from them again and prayed. But the third time he called to them: 'The hour is at hand.' "

In the anticipation of his destiny the Lord spoke again and again about his suffering and the mystery of the sacrifice. "But they understood none of these things; this saying was hid from them, and they did not grasp what was said." All discipleship is blind. Beside the denial of Peter and the flight of the disciples at the capture stands the confession of Peter and the communion of the last supper. The magical and compelling appearance of the master is always for the disciple the last support and the highest challenge; therefore, the proud triumph and the deepest fall are always so close together. The master can do everything in order to acquaint the disciples with the mysteries of the teaching; but one thing he cannot do: he cannot produce the impetus for them, the stirring of the soul by which they will be free. For Socrates, the μαιεύεσθαι [midwifery] is the highest activity; the γεννᾶν [engendering] belongs to God.

From this we learn a new tragic element in the life of the master—the knowledge that everyone has to walk the last stretch, the hardest way, alone; that he, who gives the best which he has to the men whom he loves, must leave them here—yes, even drive them away. The master takes upon himself that which is most difficult. No one is permitted to sense how difficult that is. The mysterious word of Mark sounds like an allusion to it: "Can you drink the cup which I drink? Can you be baptized with the baptism with which I am baptized?" The master waited for this impetus in the soul of the disciple. This is the interpretation of the mysterious relation between the Lord and the one who betrayed him, a silent understanding which is expressed in the imploring words of the master: "What you must do, do quickly."

It belongs to the task which the chosen one undertakes in the hour of his call to keep this greatest difficulty secret. Bertram, in the chapter significantly called "Socrates" of his beautiful book on Nietzsche, also explores this problem with reference to his hero; he discusses the final silence which is laid upon the existence of the master; indeed he goes further and speaks of the *deception* involved.

This is a Greek twist, but it points out a feature in the life of all masters. The power of the example depends upon this deception, which is, in the deepest sense, instructive. It is the secret of his power to redeem. The nature of the world, the somber truth, is recognized—and banished. The sadness, which must overpower everyone who encounters it unarmed, is checked; a redemption is found. But no one must know how difficult the struggle was, or how deep the suffering: *Bis die Lasten der Lotse zaehlt, die Leichen nicht mit*[5] (Klopstock). There is something of deception, of a tender, careful deception, in this knowing kindness, in the melancholy wisdom which the disciple experiences with the master. As the profound word of the Lord proclaims it, which he says in the Acts of John to the favorite disciple: "What you are, you will see— that, I will show to you. But what I am, that alone I know, no one else. What is mine, let it be mine; but what is yours, receive through me!"

Also in this aspect, the master's existence makes a demand; and as his whole existence is only the progressive manifestation of a deep and mysterious tragedy, there is no "master-figure" which does not disclose this in both large and small respects— this demand is dialectical from the very beginning. It is the master's will to draw close to himself and rise above himself. Therefore he demands the self-delivery of the disciple: the sacrifice of the body, of the spirit, of all his possessions. He guides him on the way; he is—here we see the transition to the teacher, indeed to the mystagogue and head of a school— the leader, the father, the rescuer. In this sharply defined

characteristic we understand the relationship in the ancient
mysteries, in Sufistic union, and in the Hindu, especially Shi-
vaistic, *guru*-practice. The πατήρ (father), the sheik, the *guru,*
the zaddick: as a guide of souls, as a door to salvation, they
demand the complete devotedness of the disciple, of the "son."
The Murid is the son of the sheik, which signifies here more
than a simple simile: "As the body is conceived in the womb
of the mother through the father's seed"—so it reads according to Ibn Arabi—"so also with the heart in a spiritual
birth." The spirit of the Murid is conceived in the womb of
his soul, through the "in-breathing" of the sheik. It is at this
birth that Isa—Jesus—was aiming with the phrase: "He who
is not born twice will not enter the kingdom of heaven." The
Murid must obey his spiritual father *perinde ac cadaver* [as
through the body]. "The true disciple," says Dhu'n Nun,
"must obey his master more than God himself."

However, here we immediately meet that other dimension:
the master points not only to himself; he also directs the
disciple away from himself. We think of Socrates, whose harsh
and severe method of wonderfully invigorating irony provides
a beautiful example of the effect on his disciple, whereby he
directs the disciple away from himself and to the disciple
himself. This is evident also when in the activity of Buddha's
instructing the disciples, a strict distance is kept which seems
to deny the later interpretation which the members of the
"Great Church" were inclined to apply to the master. How
otherwise are we to understand the synoptic accounts of the
majestic authoritative words of Jesus: "Why do you call me
good? No one is good but God alone"; even unto the requirement of faith, which implies the highest spontaneity and
activity of the soul.

Up to now our investigation has led to the consideration
of the relation between master and disciple with special regard
to the life of the master. We will now point out the two great
possibilities which a master can realize. As the most significant
historical expression of these possibilities, one might, on the
one hand, consider the ancient Greek master of the Empe-
docles-Socrates type and, on the other, the master of the

Gospels who perhaps remains the most sublime example. Søren Kierkegaard has seen the precise difference more clearly than anyone else and expressed it with the eloquence and depth peculiar to him in his *Philosophical Fragments*. It is preceded by the motto: Is a historical point of departure possible for an eternal consciousness? How can such a point of departure have any other than a mere historical interest? Is it possible to base eternal happiness upon historical knowledge?

The figure of the master lives in the heart of the disciples. So long as he dwells in their midst, the image grows and takes on form. Through this image each disciple is able to focus his own experience, which is enriched stroke by stroke from a living center. This growth occurs according to the law and rhythm of the natural reciprocal influence and the dynamic of the relation between man and man. With the exhaustion of the living fount, the process of the formation does not stop; but along with this continuing process, from now on, a petrification occurs under a different law of construction. Imagination and personal experience are replaced by productive fantasy, which continues to shape the further development of the image. The magical circle of individual life is broken through. In the interchange of dialogue and in the proclamation it becomes expanded. The "objective" character of the image, its social reception, demonstrates that it is on the way to becoming myth. With its reception it is modified in new ways: just as the individuality of the disciples was decisive for the selection, combination, and elaboration of the objective facts, so now the same conditions are effective in the contribution which everyone who seeks to perpetuate the image makes to its alteration. Love and hate shape it. Continually, this image is active, and out of its action it receives a new splendor. The enemies continually oppose it and produce thereby the "black myth," the opposite to the glorification. Jesus is a son of the Devil according to Mandaren. Schools and factions are built. The basic reason for the separation and union of adherents is the nature of the image of the master which lives in the heart. In addition to these, in a strict psychological factor, objective factors operate: tradition, inertia, assimilation, deterioration, etc. All the combining factors which are necessarily connected with the verbal and written formulation—the misunderstanding and new meaning, interpretation and stylization—enter in.

Let us illustrate this by recalling the variation, the characteristic similarities and differences of the images of Jesus according to Matthew, Mark, Luke, and John. How decisive for Paul's image of Jesus—besides the individuality of Paul— is the fact that he is a "disciple at second hand"! Is it necessary to remind one's self of the memorable example of the Platonic and Xenophonic Socrates?

Not only do the individualities influence the change of the images; it would be an important problem of the philosophy of history in the study of the history of religions to search out the influences, the categories, through which a precise "relative a priori"—to use Simmel's expression—acts upon the shaping of the "images": national, tribal, race, class, sex-membership. The wise Buddha becomes the world-savior of Mahayana, the Japanese Amitabha, the Chinese Fo; the Christ of Aryan Christians is certainly a different one from him who belongs to Syrian or Egyptian Gnosticism. Rules always govern the change of these images. Certain basic elements persist; certain features are drawn more heavily here or there. From the history of the portrayals of Christ we can perceive the fluctuation of rationalistic and mystical, worldly and eschatological, theomorphic and anthropomorphic conceptions. But all these are later speculations which presuppose the myth upon which they act in an expanding, deepening, enlarging manner and whose change they influence.

Decisive, on the one hand, is the history of the origin of the myth; it falls into the period which circumscribes the first attempt at fixing the image, on the other. Here, again, the first appearance of the disciple-at-secondhand, the follower, marks the division of the "original" fellowship from later times. To a certain degree, the first experience always remains esoteric; with the arrival and solicitation of followers, the esoteric experience becomes more or less an exoteric event. At the time of the first written formulation, however, something entirely new—a minimum criterion, so to speak—is created, to which the most daring allegories and stories, the most addicted to miracles and fantasy, must still have to conform through danger of being expelled. From here on the distinction of historical and unhistorical becomes important— a distinction which in a second stage becomes identified, emphasized, and limited by the canonical and non-canonical. We observe a similar development in the artistic portrayal, the gradual evolution of a canonical type, which always showed a differentiation effected by relative a priori as to race, epoch, country, etcetera.

The disciple's experience of the master is a social one; however much it may be differentiated in other respects, it is a form of social experience. It exhibits the laws of communities as such. The corresponding sociological category is the group *(der Bund)*, as we lately have been so beautifully shown.[6] Certain attitudes which determine the action of the members of this circle either for or against one another are applicable only out of a background of communal character. The movements of the members of the circle toward or away from one another find their meaning only in the meaning of the group. Such were the relations of the disciples as told by Mark and Luke, which have wrongly been interpreted solely as a shameful competition for supremacy. The realization of the outward constitution of this association here—be it loose or very strict—is unimportant. There will always be disciples who are closer to the master than all others, as were John and Ananda and the witnesses of Jesus' transfiguration or his last struggle. And around the smaller and smallest circle there will be another one. On a higher level the circle has the same double meaning for the master as for the disciple; it represents humanity, and it is the union of friends in which the master finds the comfort and strength which allows the lonely one to experience human fellowship. The circle is the supporting and nourishing ground out of which everyone who belongs gains his strength; it is the concrete revelation of the "power" of the master. Attracted by this power, moved by it, and defined through it, the disciples assemble in a circle around the master; followers and helpers assemble in ever wider circles. This is the power of which Goethe spoke when he said that God continually remains active in higher nature in order to draw the inferior near unto himself.

MAHĀYĀNA BUDDHISM

GENERAL READERS ARE perhaps best acquainted with the philosophy and the art of Mahāyāna—which are certainly two
essential areas of expression. However, in some ways these
two are better suited to lead one away from the study of
Mahāyāna than to bring him to it. A friend of philosophical
clarity or religious sincerity or a proponent of "classical" tastes
in art would understandably turn away from these "baroque"
manifestations with repugnance. But philosophy and art are
indeed rather secondary to the *religiosity* that feeds and fires
Mahāyāna. As matters stand, we can best come to know this
orientation through the study of the holy scriptures. To be
sure, even here we are hindered by widespread prejudices
when we want to bring our friends to the study of Mahāyāna
Buddhism. Let us examine the most popular of these prejudices.

The argument that very few people are equipped to approach the sources is invalid; many people have studied the
Hīnayāna scriptures in translation to their deepest inward
benefit and their greatest profit. But for many the Mahāyāna
scriptures are reputed to be atrociously long-winded and te-

33

dious. In this case people are usually thinking of the *Lalita-vistara* and *Mahāvastu,* the only scriptures associated with Ma-hāyāna that are also rather well-known in broader academic circles. Perhaps many people have been discouraged from reading a Mahāyāna sūtra by its—at times exceptionally ex-tensive—enumeration of names and objects, its profusion of numbers and stereotyped concepts, and its eternal repetitions. I shall later write a few more words explaining all this; but right now we must remember that ultimately every human race, every people, every religious, political, and social group has its own style of thinking and speaking. If we want to take an interest in non-Christian religions, then we must take the trouble to try and enter into this style and to understand it. To the student who has perhaps come to these writings from studies in folklore or fairy tales and who is now "disillusioned" by their long-windedness, we might say that no religious text is easy and entertaining reading. Finally, in reading such texts one must keep in mind the end to which they were written, namely, religious edification. I find that the Mahāyāna sūtras, in their own way, bear comparison with the Hīnayāna sūtras very well. But we must not make the mistake of approaching the one phenomenon with a criterion constructed from the other one and thus of wanting to judge it on the basis of an ideal which is wholly different from its own.

As for the aesthetic impression, first of all, it would nat-urally be wrong for us to expect that the Mahāyāna sūtras should have the same simplicity and unity that are in some sense proper to the sūtras of the Lesser Vehicle. Just to mention a single factor that naturally determines the character of their aesthetic form, the Mahāyāna sūtras are devoted to the ex-altation of the *Mahāpuruṣa;* unlike, for example, the literature of the southern canon, they do not praise the Buddha primarily as a *teacher* and a *man.* Even while reading certain parts of the *Majjhima-Nikāya*—not to mention any of the later or more abstract writings—much of what is presented there will seem diffuse, complicated, and verbose. But if the reader can acquire the inner composure and stillness that will permit him to penetrate the spirit of this literature, to understand it and to

enjoy it, then he will also be able to understand the style of
thinking and speaking that the Indians created for themselves.
Whoever wishes to become familiar with Mahāyāna must simply accept a much bigger criterion; he must become broader
and more open—I might say more elastic—so that he can
acquire the inner momentum that will enable him to think,
feel, and move with his subject.

When we first come into the presence of the gigantic
dimensions that dominate everything here, they take our breath
away—when we have just barely entered this world, we become
deaf, blind, and confused. Let us suppose that during a walk
through the narrow streets of a small town we were suddenly
to stand before a building the size of the cathedral at Cologne.
At first we would see nothing at all; we would have no
conception of the totality before us. If, however, we had been
prepared for such a sight, our eyes would have no difficulty
in probing and encompassing the mighty planes and heights;
then our own feelings of smallness and oppression would not
interfere with the elevating effects of such a view in the same
way as in the first instance. Once we have acquired the
momentum that permits us to breathe in India's more or less
tropical world; once we have become especially broad and
open, so that we do not shrink from even the most monstrous
of concepts, letters, and numbers, then the world of Mahāyāna
can be unveiled for us in all its beauty and sublimity. We
must first achieve an inner relationship to this whole world;
then we will be able to grasp the *inner necessity,* which rules
here as in any organic structure and which, of course, is also
involved in the problem of the relationship of content to
aesthetic form. We must be able to understand that all this
repetition and accumulation, all these colossal numbers and
spaces are not just the play of an imagination gone mad; this
is not a question of "play" at all—or if it is, then the word
must be given a very deep and philosophical meaning. Again,
just to cite a single example, the practice of formulating fixed
and stereotyped figures of speech, already reflected to a lesser
degree in the Hīnayāna scriptures, becomes here a kind of
codification of a quantity of rigid formulas which seem to

threaten all life with suffocation. Thus any reference to the Buddha is always accompanied by the same massive and rigid retinue of names and predicates. This "stylization" extends so far that even in describing the trees that might adorn the realm of a Buddha, there is talk not of ten or one hundred or even one thousand but of hundreds of tens of millions (*koṭi*) of trees—and they are not ordinary trees but trees of diamonds and other precious materials. The *Lotus* is overflowing with such examples.

What must be taken into account here is a *difference in the character of the aesthetic forms.* The great, incontestable, and immediately evident value of a noble expression, of a beautiful form, dare not be underestimated—and we are referring here not only or even primarily to its aesthetic value but above all to its religious value. Today we have again become more conscious of the significance of this kind of value in its "sociological" reference, that is, in its capacity for creating and preserving society. Cult is the nucleus of all objective religion. Surely it is not by chance that Hīnayāna has been able to win and hold only a comparatively small number of people, while even today Mahāyāna binds hundreds of millions. The Mahāyāna scriptures reflect a high degree of objective religion. It is also expressed through Mahāyāna's aesthetic forms. Today it is difficult to avert misunderstanding in using the antithesis "internal-external" because so much mischief has been done with it. Nonetheless, I should like to suggest that the form of the holy scriptures of Hīnayāna, conforming to the more introverted nature of Hīnayāna piety, is significantly more "subjective" than that of the Mahāyāna writings—a religious literature that constructs a monstrously rich, manifold, variegated, and complicated "objective" world.

Let us consider another prejudice which still frequently obstructs our appreciation of Mahāyāna Buddhism. Mahāyāna is supposed to be completely unoriginal and dependent; it is a mixture of Hinduism and Buddhism—possibly an unfortunate mixture, to be understood and interpreted only as a degeneration of the original teaching of the Buddha. No one will contest the *complex character* of this form of religiosity.

On the contrary, probably the most important and instructive work incumbent on the history of religions at the present time is the historical analysis of Mahāyāna Buddhism. Furthermore, if we consider the teachings of "original" Buddhism to be identical with the nucleus of the older sources of the Hīnayāna scriptures, then we must immediately admit that these teachings, as well as the whole "religion of Buddha," underwent a marked change in their later development; and we can readily understand how, from the standpoint of the "classical ideal" this development might be viewed as nothing but deprivation and decline. If, for the time being, we refrain from passing judgments, then all of the preceding discussion can signify only that it would be very rewarding to focus historical studies on the origins of Mahāyāna Buddhism. But we cannot deny that, no matter how great the influence of forms already in existence may have been at its inception, and no matter how complex and manifold and colorful its components may appear to be in historical analysis, Mahāyāna Buddhism is nonetheless a unique phenomenon, which we cannot "explain" by summarizing its constituent elements. For no matter how many concepts, images, and phrases were borrowed and adopted from other religions, and no matter how superficial their reception has often been, there is a new center here. We must understand the dogmas, concepts, and forms as being its modes of expression. The number of intermediate structures and transitional phenomena between Hīnayāna and Mahāyāna makes no difference; we will never circumvent the necessity of confessing that in Mahāyāna, as opposed to the "old" form, something specifically new came into being out of a basic outlook that was new—something that had its own structure and its own value.

Nor can we completely explain the novelty by talking about Buddhism's reception among non-Indian peoples, whose characteristic traits are to be made responsible for its transformation, although the findings of folk psychology would have considerable significance in an investigation of this problem. All kinds of heterogeneous "foreign influences" have been more or less unilaterally postulated in the origin of Mahāyāna.

But at the same time people have attempted to deny as many
external influences as possible and to demonstrate that Buddhism is an exclusively Indian phenomenon. Undoubtedly—
the research of de la Vallée Poussin above all has shown this—
there already existed in the oldest form of Buddhism known
to us a number of traits, at least in embryonic form, that later
attained their full development for the first time in Mahāyāna.
By its limited recognition of Hīnayāna, the Greater Vehicle
shows that its teachers did not break with the old forms. But
the transformation of the old forms was so radical that we
can readily say it would not have been possible to this degree
without an impetus from the outside.

A question relevant in this context is whether the transformation of Buddhism into Mahāyāna was effected primarily
through the intervention and influence of one or more outstanding personalities, for example, Nāgārjuna or whoever the
"founder" of Mahāyāna might be, or whether it happened
because the influence of the "masses" forced concessions and
thus brought about a change in the original religion. Here
too, there is of course no "either-or" answer; rather we must
try to ascertain the way and the degree to which both factors
actually operated. Such a discussion would also be important
because it would help to explain the remarkable and much-
noted fact that in Mahāyāna we find, beside some very crude,
coarse, and primitive beliefs, rites, and customs, the most
sublime and subtle ideas and teachings. And these, indeed,
do not only exist side by side—they are frequently mixed, as
in the peculiar piety of Tibetan Buddhism. Sublime speculations on the emptiness of things and the nature of the savior
are intermingled with the use of the prayer-wheel and a belief
in ghosts. And of course things are not so comfortably arranged
that the theoretician can find the higher speculations and more
sophisticated practice existing exclusively in the circles of the
highest spirituality—among scholars, for example—and then
observe the masses abiding in the simple spirit worship of
their fathers. Everything is intermixed and intermingled. The
historical and philosophical problem opens into that of the
sociology of religion. It is enough for us to remember the

circumstances in Japan. How was Buddhism transformed within the individual sects under the influence of the sociological structure, and how did its specific religiosity in turn affect the latter?

To many of us it may seem questionable to conceive of or to comment upon Mahāyāna Buddhism as a totality. They will point out the wealth of national differences, sects, schools, and views that are all comprehended under the name. But all of these call themselves Mahāyānist, as even today we speak of Protestantism in general, referring to the sum of those empirical phenomena that call themselves by this name. As one comes to know a great religion more and more accurately, one comes to see within it more and more significant and fundamental differences and divisions—until finally the whole readily appears to be only a "unity of contrasts." How great are the tensions which Heiler has pointed to in Catholicism and Glasenapp in Hinduism! I cannot doubt that, if the time comes when Mahāyāna Buddhism is presented as a whole, a very similar discovery will be made.

Is there such a thing as the "spirit" of Mahāyāna? Is there something that will permit us to grasp this phenomenon as a unity, are there instances that are characteristic of it, especially in the context that has been introduced here? There are three approaches, it seems to me, through which one can attempt to determine the essence of Mahāyāna Buddhism; in the areas of religion, of philosophy, and of ethics, it has set up an ideal that gives us an insight into its essence. We can learn about it if we ask first, "What is its attitude toward God?" second, "What is its attitude toward mankind?" and third, "What is its attitude toward the 'world'?" At the same time, the answers to these questions will highlight the differences between Ma-hāyāna and Hīnayāna.

First of all, however, we have to make a few *literary* remarks—especially with regard to the text from which we shall proceed.

If we would want to paint a picture of Hīnayāna Buddhism based on its scriptures, it would not be difficult. Both the Pali Canon (of which a very significant part is available to us even

in our own language) and a few works in Sanskrit inform us
about it. We even have the complete canon of a Hīnayāna
sect, the Pāli-Tipiṭaka. No complete Sanskrit canon is extant.
It is characteristic of Mahāyāna and its "henotheizing" and
bibliolatrous tendencies that each of the Mahāyāna sects usually
has its own particularly sacred book.

The crown of the Mahāyāna scriptures in all respects is
and continues to be the *Saddharma-Puṇḍarīka*.[1] The significance
of its content and its religious and aesthetic value are well
known. Unfortunately, when scholars have taken an interest
in this work it has too often been muddied by apologetic
concerns, which make impartial evaluation very difficult. It is
no accident that this was the first of the Sanskrit scriptures
of the northern school, and one of the first texts of the entire
Buddhist literature, to be translated into a European language.
In the second volume of his epoch-making *Introduction au
Bouddhisme*, Eugène Burnouf offered a translation of "Le Lotus
de la bonne loi."[2] Hendrik Kern's new English translation of
the text in 1884 was largely based on it.[3] Burnouf devoted
exceptional love and care to the work—the second half of
the second volume and the third volume consist of notes and
appendices intended to help clarify philologically, factually,
and historically some of the more important concepts of the
Saddharma-Puṇḍarīka sūtra. Even today, in spite of their many
dated suppositions and constructs, these volumes are still indispensable to the continuing study of the *Lotus*, although they
are more helpful in clarifying specific concepts than they are
in introducing and evaluating the spirit of the work.

Perhaps it would not be out of place for us to remember
a few outstanding dates in the history of a book that has been
a source of supreme wisdom for so many thousands of people.
We do not know when the *Saddharma-Puṇḍarīka* was first
written. Moriz Winternitz, who objects to Kern's predated
quotations for the earlier sources, would date the original
form of the book at about A.D. 200. Burnouf has fixed different
dates for the sections in Sanskrit prose and the Gāthas of
"mixed" Sanskrit that follow each chapter. Today it is believed
that the work originally consisted entirely of poetry, in which

short prose passages were scattered to introduce the verse and to bind it together. Then, as the language of the poetry became obsolete, the prose passages were expanded. Without exactly being a commentary, they undertook an explanation. The work was translated into Chinese several times—these dates are generally accepted. The first Chinese translator was Dharmarakṣa (265–316); an incomplete translation by an unknown author is equally old. Kumārajīva followed (384–417); contemporary with his translation is a Tibetan version. The translation by Jñānagupta and Dharmagupta is dated 601. In the meantime, Vasubandhu wrote a commentary on the *Saddharma-Puṇḍarīka*.

The book, as we have it, consists of twenty-seven chapters which are very unequal in length. Chapters 21 through 26 are later additions; this has been proved on the basis of internal and external evidence. Thus the older text includes Chapters 1 through 20 and Chapter 27, which serves as an epilogue. According to Kern and Winternitz, the remainder would have been added around 250 as *Pariśiṣṭas* (addenda).

In translation, the work is not excessively difficult, even for the reader who is not well-versed in this literature. Compensating for the long and boring enumerations of names and numbers which we have already talked about are the entirely unique and beautiful similes scattered throughout the book. They are of the highest religious, ethical, and aesthetic value. In fact, this is what is so singular about this work; again and again, beside many things that are "late," that is, superficial, sophistic, and scholastic, we find in it much that is simple and straightforward, reflecting genuine sensitivity. On the whole, we cannot deny that it has a highly meaningful human content. It reveals genuine wisdom, genuine goodness, genuine piety. The good doctor, the anxious father, and the wise leader are figures that are eternally human; they come to us and accompany us; they have something to say to every one of us. Who would not put up with many things that seem odd, exaggerated, or circumstantial—with many things that to us, born under a different sun and in a different time, seem to be tasteless or even laughable—for the sake of human enrichment and of aesthetic and religious elevation? In spite of the hieratic and ceremoniously rigid style of the work, is there not a great deal of life here—life in the people whose words we hear, and whose acts we witness, and life above all in the Buddha Śākyamuni and in the great disciples who have been transformed into archangels?

I

Now let us discuss briefly Mahāyāna's attitude toward God, toward mankind, and toward the world.

Traditionally, people have considered "atheism" to be one of the chief characteristics of the teaching of the Buddha according to the Lesser Vehicle. This view is doubtless correct. Another feature often emphasized in addition to atheism is its autosoteriology, the belief that each individual stands on his own feet and must accomplish his own salvation. The discoverer of the way to salvation thus has only a minimal role.

The old gods of Brahmā-heaven recede completely into the background; where they appear, they are *dii otiosi*, they are one class of the beings which are all in need of salvation through the Buddha. By the time of the Buddha, little remained of the once important and powerful Vedic gods who had again and again interfered in the life of the individual. The era of the Brāhmaṇas and Upaniṣads had developed a *Weltanschauung* that left no room for personal creators and world-destroyers or for good and evil lords. Its worldview substituted for lordship an impersonal and blind fate; man could only acknowledge its regularity and seek to escape it. This philosophy or metaphysic led immediately to an ethic, and the ethic was identical with the teaching of salvation. For the most part, the older form of Buddhism adopted this worldview, although it introduced many important changes. The most decisive one is that *personal power* was once again conceded a place in the system. In the Upaniṣads, salvation had remained a task that was uniquely and entirely the accomplishment of the individual person. All community and all leadership in the deeper sense of the word were hopelessly excluded from this individualistic and aristocratic system. The teaching of the Upaniṣads is more of a philosophy than a religion. But even though the older Buddhism remained very much aware of its fundamentally autosoteriological conceptions, it also recognized that the Buddha was decisive as the leader to salvation. We must bear in mind what a radical alteration was implied for the worldview when even the supreme law which regulated everything appeared to have been ruptured at a certain point, in that decisive moment when the Bodhisattva attained enlightenment. Here the ethic, which in Buddhism is also identical with the teaching of salvation— perhaps even more than it had been in the Brāhmaṇic system— has much more latitude; it has a task that is metaphysically meaningful—suspending at *one* point the cosmic law, unraveling it, as it were. But, as we have said, what is most decisive is the reinstitution of the *leader-personality*.

To be sure, there are many different opinions concerning the role assigned to the Buddha in the oldest form of Buddhism. Even the texts do not give us any wholly unified body of information. On the one hand, people like to quote the words of the dying master which have been handed down to us in the *Mahāparinibbāna-Sūtra*.[4] On the other hand, we have evidence testifying to the "uniqueness" of the savior. The much-noted cool and abstract way of thinking of the oldest Buddhism surely corresponds very well to the figure of a master who fundamentally had no metaphysical nobility that would in any way have elevated him above the other creatures. At that time men probably saw in the Buddha only a teacher who had attained release and who taught release as a *primus inter pares*. For all that, he was as such still distinguished in the eyes of his disciples from the many lesser teachers of salvation who lived and worked around him, for he claimed to be the *first*—without a "model"—to have found this salvation. This must have distinguished him from all the other teachers, who were always aspiring to deliverance in the sense of the *Karma-* or *Jñāna-mārga* or according to some other "instruction." We find in the southern canon a codification of the teachings of the Buddha and ideas about his appearance which strongly emphasize characteristics that are rationalistic and individualistic. We have no reasons for doubting that many things pointing in this direction were in fact present in the proclamation of the master. On the other hand, it is in my opinion entirely wrong to want to interpret the rise of Mahāyāna only in terms of its opposition, its contradiction, or its reaction to Hīnayāna. The most important motives and factors at work in its development are of an interior and "necessary" nature. In any religion with a founder there develops within a certain length of time a cult of the founder. We cannot here attempt to search out the objective and psychological motives behind this fact. But it is noteworthy that some tendencies in this direction developed even in southern Buddhism, as indicated by the *Nidānakathā* and, generally speaking, by the *Jātaka*. De la Vallée Poussin, who has done us the great service of keeping precisely this continuity in mind and of dealing with it, has—following Minayeff, Foucher, and others—thoroughly studied the *Lokottaravādin* texts in light of their significance for the understanding of the "transitions." These texts adhere to a supernatural conception of the Buddha, without considering themselves to be Mahāyānist. A few more words must be said on this point.

I believe that we should accustom ourselves to the idea that there may have been men among the disciples and followers of Śākyamuni whose experience of the Buddha was very different from that of the men whose spirit speaks to us out of the canon of the South. And surely these men were not only the poor and the simple in spirit, not only the listeners on the fringes who were not capable of grasping the "true meaning" of the Buddha's teaching or their like. We must realize that disciples of the Buddha—and especially the most significant of them—were not types; they were individual people. It has correctly been said that the great disciples all look alike in the scriptures; Hermann Oldenberg once said that they are not persons, they are the incarnate common spirit of the Buddha's disciples. I think that this is an interesting observation which shows us the direction in which we are to look. The work of redacting and canonizing has already been done here; *we* stand before its *results*. It is obvious that the sects of the Pali Canon stylized the portrayal of the disciples no less than they did that of the master—in their own way. But others have also drawn their pictures, and we can learn from their portrayals how they understood the appearance of the master and his disciples and the teaching.

Let us consider the circle of Socrates or that of Jesus. No one will deny that in the writings of Plato and Xenophon or in the Gospels we have "portrayals" which show us the figure of a master as seen through a temperament. They involve more than a temperament, of course; they have been comprehended and molded by an individuality. To be sure, things are different in India insofar as the type predominates there and the individual elements disappear—as Oldenberg has correctly emphasized. But of course individual variations did and do exist. It just happens that people do not consider them to be what is ultimately important; on the contrary, it is the general that is essential. All variations from the norm are evaluated negatively. Moreover, the philosophical and historical idea of orderliness obviously would also have had some influence on the origin and the career of the portrayals. Without saying more, it is evident that men of different natures would have come together in a circle like those which the great masters, including the Buddha, gathered around themselves. If one were to question each of the disciples about his experience of the master, he would find that crucial differences would come to light already in the experience itself, that is to say, in the perception of it, and that further significant differences would appear in the way of formulating an expression of that experience. Thus, for example, in spite of the fact that we can presuppose in every instance a certain "will to clarification," a "realist" on such an occasion outlines a different picture from that of the "idealist," and so on. Can anyone doubt that a report on Jesus by Peter would have been different—would have had to be different from one by John or Andrew or by any of the other disciples? Would not an Ānanda have seen and loved "another" Buddha than the Buddha of Ajñāta Kauṇḍinya or of any other man? And what holds true for the immediate disciples would of course be true to an even higher degree for those who followed after them, for all the "pupils and followers." To be sure, it is difficult even in the Gospels of the New Testament to extricate and to distinguish individual characteristics and to separate that which is late and worked over from the precipitate of the primary impression. To undertake such a project with the sources of Buddhism must seem to be almost impossible. We must remember moreover the Indian aversion, already mentioned, to anything singular, abnormal, or individual. The kind of work that has achieved such rich results in the study of the New Testament canon can never be exercised on the Buddhist scriptures. Rather we must attempt to make as clear as possible the forms of this experience in their manifoldness and their differences. And that which we have said up to now about the master also holds true in many respects for the tradition of the teaching in the more limited sense of the word. Here too we know comparatively little about the individual traditions that must have circulated before and after the codification. But even if many remnants did not allude to them, we would have to infer their existence from studying the historical and philosophical presuppositions of the development of the objective religious establishments. We are not at all prejudging anything about chronology, that is, about establishing the dates of the teachers and writings of the Mahāyāna schools—their roots are in the earliest times; rather we are trying to give the psychological and objective points of departure in which the speculations of the later schools were grounded and out of which they are therefore to be understood. We cannot explain any "variation" with the aid of "time" alone—then, for example, there would be no reason for the earlier Hīnayāna to have persisted alongside the later Mahāyāna; rather we must take into consideration the great range of inner possibilities which existed from the very beginning.

Scholars have rightly paid attention to the "pre-education" that must be posited for most of the Buddha's disciples and audience. Were there not adherents of many different orientations among them, yogins and ascetics of every conceivable kind? Thus many of the ideas and categories which they brought with them to their experience of the Buddha gave direction to the development of the existing tradition and above all assisted in its codification and systematization.[5] When the dogmatics applied the predicate *Mahāpuruṣa* to the Buddha—as we know, the *Mahāpuruṣa* is characterized by a number of specific primary and secondary physical and spiritual attributes—or that of *Cakravartin*—this does not imply, as de la Vallée Poussin has already and very appropriately remarked, that they were "idealizing" or recalling attributes of the historical Śākyamuni. Rather they were utilizing certain terms out of the treasury of preformulated concepts to give expression to the still living—perhaps still immediate—impression of the majesty and divinity of the Buddha. It is neither by chance nor by caprice that they adopted precisely those concepts which had originally been filled with a different content. Such concepts offered a perception of the appearance of the Buddha in which the experience "Buddha" was not exhausted in the appearance of the teacher; rather they were grounded in the (religious) experience of a "supernatural" manifestation.

We are accustomed—and the texts of the southern canon encourage us in this direction—to viewing the Buddha as a good and sublimely tranquil man. But now we have seen that he could also be experienced as *Mahāpuruṣa* or *Mahāsattva*. The ideas expressed in these and in similar dogmatic formulations must in time have spread further and further. A certain explanation by de la Vallée Poussin is very interesting in this connection; in it he shows how identical terms might have been understood in both realistic and supernaturalistic ways. *Mahāsattva* could have implied divinity, but it could also have designated someone (human) of a superior nature. There were "minimizers" who interpreted, for example, Śākyamuni's saying that he would remain in the world until the end of this *kalpa* to mean that he would remain for a human lifetime, that is, for a hundred years. Later on, as the tradition and the teaching gradually developed and took on form, the different tendencies which had been present from the very beginning—let us call them the realistic and supernatural tendencies, although the difference in meaning would have been great—must inevitably have become unwieldy and thus incapable of being expressed through a unified terminology. If the extreme realists would already have had reservations about a middle-of-the-road understanding which was only colored by supernaturalism, as perhaps reflected in the *Lokottaravādin*, then extremely supernatural conceptions such as those found in the writings of the Mahāyāna teachers must have aroused their deepest displeasure. On the other hand, we can thoroughly understand that those minds that had, in accordance with their nature and experience, known the Buddha to be God could not have been satisfied with a moderately "supernatural" understanding like that expressed in the three sections of the *Nidānakathā*—not to mention the teachings of the Sthaviras.

It is necessary for us to distinguish between the basic conception, which is for the most part very old, and the dogmatic formulations of the respective schools, sects, and branches that developed the original teachings and in time organized, refined, or coarsened them. Often we do not recognize the predispositions already present in the origins until their final consequences have been drawn. Thus, although the formulation of the theory of a simultaneous plurality of Buddhas was of course a late development, nonetheless even here the idea of absolute "uniqueness" was ruptured by the recognition of a number of Buddhas preceding Śākyamuni. When we come to the supernaturalists of the Greater Vehicle each scripture outdoes the other. The Buddhas are infinitely multiplied in time and in space. There are hundreds of millions of them. There are countless Buddha-realms, each of them comprehending multimillions of worlds. Thus countless Buddhas are reigning in any given second. This is Mahāyāna. How can we understand such concepts? Might not all of this be simply an invasion of the old Hindu pantheon or the unbridled license of a mad imagination playing with faces and, ultimately, only with names and numbers?

We can probably characterize the central experience of Mahāyāna, as far as content is concerned, as follows: it is the discovery that there is (a) God. Was the founder and the master of Buddhism this God? He was also God, but this God was not manifest in him alone. He is revealed through countless manifestations. It is said that the pantheon of Mahāyāna is very large. Who is the greatest among these—gods? We do not wish to ask such a question, for it reflects a perspective peculiar to our own way of thinking. The pious Mahāyāna Buddhist may rejoice in an abundance of manifestations of the Divine. In prayer to each of them he pours out the fullness of his devotion to God. In back of all of them there stands the Dharmakāya, the true Being, which is concretized in the Tathāgata. We have seen that what was decisive in the appearance of the Buddha as against the teaching of the Upaniṣads was the reintroduction of personal power into the worldview of the Indians; the thought of help, of merciful help, was thoroughly impressed upon them. In the preaching of the Buddha it probably remained in the background. The older Buddhism of the Pali texts permits it to play only an insignificant role. But there came a time when this thought— which perhaps only a few had at first grasped with enthusiasm—became the consolation of millions. Even if it had been unimportant in the Master's preaching, had not the very appearance of the Buddha been a manifestation of "help"? And now this thought was quickened with the religious ardor characteristic of the Indian people and was grasped with enormous intensity. This merciful help must be great, infinitely great, and near, infinitely near. There is no more living expression for the intensity with which this thought was thought than the godhead of Mahāyāna—incessantly multiplying, always clothing itself in new manifestations, always descending anew into the world of men, always prepared for new sacrifices. We could hardly wish to interpret this pluralistic perception of God as monotheism, nor are we referring to the late and philosophically abstract speculation on the *Ādi-Buddhas*. Merciful, saving love—this is Śākyamuni, this is Amitābha or Amitāyus, as well as the many others who can often be differentiated from one another only by name. This is the breath and the substance of those beings who have been specifically created by the Mahāyāna belief—the Bodhisattvas. We meet most of these great deities in the *Saddharma-Puṇḍarīka*. At its center, however, is the Buddha Śākyamuni. In other Mahāyāna sūtras it is more often Amitābha who appears as "God"—as we have said, for the believer such a change creates no problems. It is not just a matter of his being tolerant and broad-minded in regard to his own life and that of the stranger; what is decisive for him is the fact that there is a helpful deity whom he will call upon now as Śākyamuni, now as Amitābha, as he prefers. To be sure, the veneration of the Buddha Amitābha has drawn those who seek the help of this god into a closer union. He has an exuberant cult, and many sects follow this particular form of the Mahāyāna teaching. It has rightly been said of the Amida religion that it is *bhakti-mārga*; here all commands are subordinated to one—the believer must put his faith and trust in Amitābha who, as a result of his especially high and merciful vow, is now enthroned as the king of Sukhāvatī, the western land of the blessed.

In the *Saddharma-Puṇḍarīka*, the Buddha Śākyamuni is called God. The sūtra wishes to show him to us in his total splendor. Thus he is enthroned in immeasurable glory on the heavenly Gṛdhrakūṭa surrounded by a heavenly audience in whom all the categories of beings are represented. If we permit this proclamation of the Buddha to work upon us, we are powerfully reminded of two of Rudolf Otto's characteristics of the Holy—"majestas" and "augustum." We feel something of the "Power" of the Lord of the World which corresponds to man's feeling of his own lowliness, insignificance, and finitude. It is the *sanctum* which man knows to exist over against himself. Otto has rightly emphasized that the awe that introduces itself in this connection is not merely a kind of fear before that which is overpowering; the *tu solus sanctus* is also a song of praise, which "so far from being merely a faltering confession of the divine supremacy, recognizes and extols a value, precious beyond all conceiving.''[6]

This is evident here. And something else is very important—the "awe" which the majesty of the Buddha arouses in us is not just a consequence of our awareness of his deeds, as is the case in Hīnayāna where the Buddha is venerated because of his great accomplishment. Contrary to the rationalistic strains in Buddhist thought, for which the impetus to admiration and worship is grounded in the knowledge of the Buddha's capacities, here, beside and before anything else, the nonrational comes into its own; the numinous makes itself felt and demands a response that is spontaneous and not based on rational deliberation. This is to say, the ethical supremacy of the Buddha—his matchless love and compassion—is not the final or the exclusive basis for his worship. What distinguishes the Lord even before his supreme moral worthiness is something other, which makes men shudder even when they only perceive the presence of the Buddha from afar. In other respects, the *Saddharma-Puṇḍarīka* is no more "monotheistic" than is Mahāyāna in general. The "majesty" is not concentrated only in the figure of the Buddha Śākyamuni—although in contrast to other sūtras it also focuses on him—rather, as we have already intimated, it rests also upon the *Tathāgatas* who come before the "present" Lord *and* after him, the great Bodhisattvas whom we have already mentioned. Perhaps it is worth pointing out, in order to avoid misunderstanding, that the description of majesty, which is intended to make us capable of seeing it and to lead us to it, is not like that of the Old or even the New Testament. There is no strong emphasis on the unique and the individual—no Rembrandt-like concentration of light on the figure who stands in the center; here the technique used is "duplication"—multiplication and integration. We cannot deny that the endless repetitions and all the other artifices whose aesthetic significance we have already pointed out are wholly suited to arouse an impression of solemn sublimity and numinous presence. Thus these long series of words create in us an effect like that of the eternally identical strophes of a litany, attuning the mind to solemnity and devotion.

A similar effect is produced by the dialogue—the "dramatic performance," according to Kern—characteristic of the *Saddharma-Puṇḍarīka*. But through the dialogue the strict solemnity is once again reinvested with life; it builds a bridge, so to speak, to the Master who is enthroned in his majesty. When a voice reaches him, and when he raises his own, men are again drawn nearer to the Buddha, and a glimmer of "humanity" is again lent to him. The dry schema theism-pantheism does little to help one appreciate the theology and the piety of the *Lotus*. The *Saddharma-Puṇḍarīka* is a fine example of the type of piety in which the "Thou" and the "He" in man's relationship[7] to God are united—not mixed. Each comes into its own—the awe before the majesty of the "He" and the trusting and devoted dependence of the creature on the "Thou" (Father).[8] Corresponding to them on the side of the Godhead are the throne in its divine glory and the love, the friendly concern for the children. The latter is particularly well expressed through the concept of the *upāya-kauśalya* of the Buddha.[9] Again and again we are illumined in new ways and on new levels which the *Tathāgata* has devised in accordance with his vow, the greatest act of his compassion, to awaken and to save men who are suffering and in error. The sūtra is inexhaustibly rich with deep and fine similes which express this anxious love.[10] The wisdom of the *Tathāgata* is so high, his knowledge is so deep, that to the man who is blind, erring, and engrossed in the world it must seem to be absolutely incomprehensible.[11] However—and what Mahāyāna shows to us is the highest reconciliation between God and man—this compassionate love turns to each man with the appropriate means and in unique ways in order to show him that he too has within himself the potential not only of ending his own suffering but also of one day being himself transformed from one saved to a savior, a *Tathāgata*. This thought binds together two diametrically opposed ideas—that of the majesty and glory of God, and that of the "deification" of men. In the Mahāyāna of the *Saddharma-Puṇḍarīka* the two are reconciled.

II

The central experience that determines Mahāyāna piety also determines its ethic—the experience of (a) God, the idea of merciful help. The decided contrast between Mahāyāna and Hīnayāna is thereby also defined for this area; Mahāyāna is heterosoteriological rather than autosoteriological. This is affirmed with all its consequences. Two consequences above all are drawn from the idea of heterosoteriology. First, it is said— somewhat in contrast to the teaching of the southern school— that the significance of the one who leads men to salvation is exemplary. Not the teaching of the Buddha but—stressing the idea of personal power—his conduct, his life are decisive. The criterion for the individual's deeds lies not in himself but in the Buddha. It follows that the highest command can no longer be the attainment of individual salvation—as Pali Buddhism formulates the goal of its way of life—but rather the imitation of the Buddha, who in turn is understood to be not merely a model for the attainment of one's own salvation, in the Hīnayānist autosoteriological sense, but a universal world savior. Thus in the ethical system of Mahāyāna the "Other" receives a distinctive significance. The Other is first of all a master and a model, and specific tasks and duties arise from this perception—emulation, veneration, adoration, service. Second, the Other is in need of help, and again specific tasks and duties arise in this connection—above all, compassion. Thus the "formal principle" that dominates the Mahāyāna ethic is the idea of imitation. Mahāyāna also knows a Nirvāṇa. This is one of the chief factors that enables all of Buddhism to consider itself a unity. However, true to the idea of imitation, the goal of the "conduct" prescribed by the Mahāyāna ethic can never be to attain this Nirvāṇa (whose precise nature is still unknown to us) as quickly as possible. In general, the Mahāyānist questions the possibility of attaining Nirvāṇa within

a single existence. Mahāyānacaryā is Bodhisattvacaryā. To a
supernatural conception of the Buddha there must also cor-
respond a supernatural conception of the discovery that marked
the high point in his life. In the Hīnayānist teaching, as we
know, the content of the Buddha's knowledge is the Fourfold
Truth and the Eightfold Path; there is nothing "supernatural"
about it. To the Mahāyāna Buddhist, this knowledge is somewhat different.[12] It is an all-embracing and all-penetrating
omniscience which is higher than all reason. Even the Buddha
could not attain it in a single night as the fruit of a single
meditation; it required infinite exertion throughout many existences. And because the true Buddhist imitates the Buddha,
he must also strive after this omniscience and begin the career
of a Bodhisattva. The one who is on the right Way is not the
Arhat, not the Pratyeka-Buddha, who is trying to win as soon
as possible for himself and by his own strength the Truth
that was once discovered by the Teacher. It is the Bodhisattva,
who is striving after Buddhahood on the difficult Path of the
ten stages. From this perspective, the disciple of the Lesser
Vehicle must seem to be an egotist—"what does his holiness
mean to me, if he is holy only for himself," asks Śāntideva's
Bodhicaryāvatāra, the ethical mirror of Mahāyāna. He is lacking
the one thing that characterizes the Buddha of Mahāyāna—
love, and specifically a positive, active love. It is evident that
the Hīnayānist's imperturbable striving after his own salvation
must seem to the Mahāyānist to be highly inconsistent. The
"I" wants freedom—but is it not true that nullifying
the "I" is one of the first demands of the Buddha, and did
not he himself act quite differently? Compassionate love marked
his career from the *Urzeit* on; whoever wishes to follow him
must learn and practice this love. Through love the Buddha
was able to acquire the means of bringing the world to salvation. He acquired the Buddha-knowledge and thus an insight
into the true nature of things; and he was thereby enabled,
first, to reveal the goal to men and, second, to acquire a
treasury of merits through which he could practice the Way
for them. Thus it is necessary for one who would follow the
Buddha to prepare himself in two ways—with the equipment

of knowledge *(jñānasaṃbhāra)* and the equipment of merit *(puṇyasaṃbhāra)*. It is necessary to practice the "perfections" or virtues through which one becomes a Bodhisattva.

Now, it should not surprise anyone who knows the Buddhism of the Pali texts that *knowledge* is an aid to salvation. But how does the concept of merit fit into Buddhism? It is understandable only in the light of Mahāyāna's world of beliefs, but in that context it makes a good deal of sense. Whatever is accomplished by compassionate love cannot be lost. Mahāyāna knows that it is possible for one to forgo enjoying the fruits of his good deeds for the sake of others. The Buddha did it and the Bodhisattva does it after him. Thus the merit of the being who has worked his way up to a higher level reverts to man: this is the consummation of the thought of merciful help. It could not be further from the kind of thinking that, oriented to the salvation of the individual soul, wants to lock up the "I" in its own special realm, denying both its obligation to others and its claim on others. At the same time it represents the most complete nullification of the "I" with its "I"-possessed world of thoughts and wishes. Nothing happens for one's own profit, but everything is for the sake of others: "to do good not for the sake of heavenly rewards, but to help the creatures; to covet Buddhist knowledge and sanctity in order to give to the ignorant and sinful."[13] Like the Holy Universal Buddhas, the Bodhisattvas who follow after them take upon themselves the heaviest burdens in order to serve all suffering creatures. They forgo an early entry into Nirvāṇa and resolve to wander over and over again through many ages and many existences. They take the vow which Śākyamuni took—to become a perfect Buddha, for only such a Buddha can save mankind. They heap merit upon merit for the sake of all—they do not even spare their own bodies, as we are shown by the magnificent example of the Bodhisattva Sarvasattvapriyadarśana in the *Lotus.*[14]

How can we describe the career of the Bodhisattva—a subject to which the *Saddharma-Puṇḍarīka* also makes constant reference? De la Vallée Poussin, our best authority on these matters, has discussed it in many places. We shall follow his description, summarizing that which is most important for our purposes.[15] In the first step, the disciple, acting either on his own or under the guidance of a master, reflects on the advantages of the Bodhi-vow, performs good works in order to free his soul, and finally takes the Bodhi-vow (praṇidhi). All this gives rise to "Enlightenment Thoughts" and makes the young man a beginner (ādikarmika). Thus there is first of all a time of preparation for the prospective Bodhisattva, during which his disposition toward Bodhisattvahood is strengthened and he directs his thoughts toward the vow that he will one day recite. Above all, it is during this period that the wish to become a Buddha ripens in him. This can be aroused in various ways. Perhaps some preacher has called the disciple; perhaps he thinks about the miraculous "body" of the Buddha; perhaps he is moved by compassion for the suffering creatures. At this stage the Buddha-thought is still subject to fluctuation and interruption. The good works are still few in number; they still require conscious deliberation and decision. There is still a considerable gap between "willing" and "doing." During three periods the aspirations of the disciple are purified. First comes the time of the "future Bodhisattva" whose stages of development can first in any proper sense of the word be called bhūmi (stories or stages). They are, respectively, the Gotrabhūmi, in which, just as the embryo carries within itself the potentiality of what it will become, so the future Bodhisattva already exists in potentiality—above all, he is good and without hate—and the Adhimukticaryābhūmi, in which the "dispositions" begin to bear fruit and the "aspirations" begin to sprout. After this time of preparation there follow the ten stages of Bodhisattvahood proper. In the first stage, the "Joyful," the candidate becomes a true Bodhisattva—as a future Bodhisattva, he had still been an ordinary man—and enters into his supernatural career (lokottarapati). It is realized through the growth of the Buddha-thought (cittopāda) which is an expression of pure compassion. By this time the latter has become fixed and enduring. It no longer fluctuates as it did during the time of preparation. It becomes the determinative and immutable vow that leads to Buddhahood *(sambodhipārāyaṇa)*. The five terrors[16] disappear for the one who has taken the sins of all beings upon himself. From now on the Holy One will experience no more evil rebirths. In the next stage he binds himself by the eight resolves *(mahāpraṇidhāna)*. These include, for example, paying homage to the Buddhas, proclaiming the Teaching, and bringing all beings to Buddhahood. At the third and fourth levels the Bodhisattva purifies this stage, in which he has acquired a number of qualities which in turn will enable him to ascend higher and higher. Among the latter are faith, compassion, good will, indefatigability, acquaintance with the books of the Teaching, reverence for himself and for others, worship of the Buddhas, etcetera. Because his love has been strong, and because they once took a vow to remain visible to those who would follow them, the Bodhisattva of the next stage is permitted to enjoy the sight of the Buddhas. He worships them and helps all creatures and in this way brings both the latter and himself to maturity. At the next level he becomes the ruler of a "continent." As he advances, he exchanges this lordship for rule over the increasingly more beautiful and more extensive realms of each of the *pāramitās*. But the Bodhisattva, liberated from all egotism, now frees all the creatures from it. The seventh *bhūmi* is "Power." Whatever the Bodhisattva does is accompanied by the following thought, "May I become the first of beings [that is, a Buddha], so that every creature may take refuge in me." The Bodhisattva is successful in whatever he does. He possesses miraculous powers, by means of which he converts untold multitudes; he lives for hundreds of *kalpas* [ages] and displays hundreds of Buddha-bodies, attains unheard-of knowledge and accomplishes unheard-of wonders. Thus he completes the "active" career of the first seven stages and prepares himself for the career of knowledge and of supernatural virtue *(jñānābhijñācaryā)*. From now on his knowledge and the depth of his meditation will be equal to his "merit." In the eighth, the "Immovable" stage, the Bodhisattva is inwardly so detached from all the activity of the world that he seems to be approaching Nirvāṇa. In accordance with a vow which they had taken as Bodhisattvas, the Buddhas

remind him of what he must still acquire before reaching Buddhahood (the ten powers and the four abilities) and of the conversions which he must still bring about. Therefore, the Bodhisattva remains in existence and performs miracles— without activity, strictly speaking. He is now capable of infinitely multiplying himself and knows and surveys the universe to which he descends in various magical forms. The Bodhisattva attains the ninth stage, the stage of the "Good Ones," by appropriating the knowledge called *pratisaṃvid;* he perfects his knowledge of the proclamation of the Teaching (*pratibhāna*). The tenth stage is called "the Cloud of the Dharma." The Bodhisattva has now become worthy of the royalty of the Teaching, through which one becomes equal to the Buddha. He lets fall the rain of the Teaching. He attains the most profound level of meditation; he achieves countless "deliverances," as well as magical formulas and powers. He is still a Bodhisattva and pays homage to the Buddhas, but he is a Bodhisattva who has become Tathāgata.

Thus the Buddha-thought has borne its finest fruit. The vow is perfectly fulfilled. We are reminded of the great songs of praise in the *Saddharma-Puṇḍarīka,* in which the Buddha reveals to all the Bodhisattvas who have completed the course their destiny to supreme and perfect enlightenment.[17]

At this point we must ask: What, actually, are the perfections that give rise to the Buddha-thought and bring it to ripeness? They fall into two groups, that of knowledge and that of merit. Essentially, the decisive virtue is *prajñā.* It is strengthening *prajñā* that contributes most to the destruction of the seeds of existence. One must guard against thinking that this knowledge is something wholly, or even only predominantly, "rational."

At this point it should be made clear that Mahāyāna demands, besides the ethical virtues and abilities, something purely "spiritual." That "spiritual" something, above all else, makes the Bodhisattva career possible and, as the *Lotus* tells us again and again, constitutes both its reward and its highest goal. The other virtues—charity (*dāna*), compassion (*karuṇā*), morality (*śīla*), patience (*kṣānti*), energy (*vīrya*), meditation *(dhyāna)*—are to be valued only when their end is the attainment of Buddhahood. This qualification helps us to understand the great significance of intentionality as a factor in the assessment of the ethical value or merit of an act. It also explains the distinction made between natural virtue *(laukika)*—whose exercise is unguided by knowledge—and supernatural virtue *(lokottara)*—which it becomes when knowledge illumines and defines it. It also becomes evident in this connection that omniscience, the supreme knowledge according to Mahāyāna, is not something that is individually and egotistically centered. It is authenticated in the act that builds a bridge to one's fellow man.

Charity is the humblest but also the most important of the virtues; strictly speaking, it is charity that gives rise to the "Buddha-thought." Charitable compassion consists of liberality, alms-giving, affability, kindness, and participation in the joy and sorrow of others. In exercising such compassion, one is even permitted to violate the other prescriptions. We are told, however, that it must not be unreasonable or excessive. Spiritual gifts as, for example, proclaiming the Teaching, are more highly valued than any of the others. The second most important virtue is morality, and in this respect Mahāyāna emphasizes "positive" conduct in addition to the negative abstinence of the southern school. At the heart of such conduct is self-respect—the preacher's endeavor to keep constant guard over the condition of his body and soul, to prevent the unjust act and to promote the good deed. For the Bodhisattva, impatience and anger are the greatest sins. Anger originates in dissatisfaction as the latter, in turn, originates in pleasure and displeasure. This feeling must be conquered through patience, which consists both of steadfastness in enduring sorrow and injustice and of knowledge of the Truth. By coming to know the cause and the nature of suffering, and thus also of anger, we are able to overcome them. Then, too, the enemy is entitled to love. Energy is also necessary if one would succeed in equipping oneself with merit and knowledge. Its enemies are weakness of the body and the spirit, attachment to the pleasures of the world, discouragement, and its consequence, self-contempt. One conquers the latter by meditating on the dangers to which one is exposed, by despising pleasure, and by keeping in mind the career of the Buddha, from its beginning in the humblest existence to its culmination in the highest knowledge. To increase his energy, the Buddha exercises his "armies": desire for the good; pride in his task, in his power, and in his endurance and pride against the passions; joy in his work and in the measure and free disposition of his strength; abandonment to the battle against the passions; and self-mastery. The final virtue is contemplation or meditation. It presupposes isolation of the body—the life of solitude—and the mind as well as indifference to all worldly pleasures. It creates a condition in which the mind is enabled to penetrate the thoughts to which it is applied and thus to be penetrated by them. The perfection of contemplation consists of practicing the *dhyāna* and *sampatti* of ancient Buddhism. It involves studying the holy truths and meditating on the impurity of the passions: in meditating on friendliness—in order to destroy hate; in meditating on dependent origination—to disperse error; and, finally, in studying all the teachings concerned with the nature of things. Thus the spirit is purified and "made free."

Just as exercising the *puṇya* virtues requires the direction of knowledge, so knowledge must also be nourished by compassion. By means of such dispositions and activities—and this concept is important for characterizing Mahāyāna—the "field" of the Bodhisattva is "purified." That is to say, he creates in and around himself an atmosphere in which the supreme virtues prosper, and in which the Bodhi-thought can grow to ripeness. Thus the virtues of merit produce the "natural body" of the Bodhisattva (*rūpakāya*); but the equipment of knowledge effects the Dharma-Being (*dharmakāya*), in which everything divine is one. And with it the circle is closed.

III

In conclusion, let us briefly sketch our third topic—the philosophy of Buddhism, or its way of looking at the world.

It is seldom expressed in the *Saddharma-Puṇḍarīka*. At present, relatively few of the source texts from which we can obtain information about this most difficult subject have been made accessible to us. Nonetheless, Western scholars from Burnouf and Wassilijew to de la Vallée Poussin and Walleser time and again have directed their attention to the philosophical problems of Mahāyāna. The difficulty is great for a number of reasons. Beyond the linguistic prerequisite, the researcher needs philosophical training to help him understand both the entire way of looking at things and the individual concepts. On the other hand, nothing could be more dangerous than importing Western ideas into the subject matter or working with categories adopted from the history of Western philosophy. Western philosophy is based on presuppositions different from those of Indian, Chinese, or Japanese philosophy and it has developed along different lines.

It has often and rightly been said that southern Buddhism, as it is reflected in the Pali canon, is hostile to metaphysics. In spite of the great role that philosophical debate plays in the *Abhidhamma* and *Sutta-Piṭaka*, the Buddha—in the mirror of the writings—remains agnostic. We shall never learn what the historic Buddha thought about such things, but it is probably not hasty of us to assume that he only rarely and never clearly discussed philosophical and especially metaphysical questions. Surely there were also men and circles in ancient Buddhism and in the southern school who were especially concerned about the philosophical exploration, establishment, and development of the Teaching—the third basket of the canon bears witness to them. But on the whole, in Pali Buddhism, philosophical and metaphysical concerns are subordinated to ethical and psychological interests. It is certainly no accident that psychological questions again and again come to the fore in Hīnayāna Buddhism; its individualistic and subjectivistic orientation is also illustrated by its great liking for the analysis and classification of mental processes. Thus no comprehensive philosophy ever developed out of the teaching, which was fundamentally positivistic and ultimately hostile to metaphysics. The practical interest, which outweighed everything else in this branch of Buddhism, was too strong. In Mahāyāna everything is different. The theoretical interest visibly grew during the course of its development and dogmatic formulation. It is true that certain of the schools continued to be exclusively or predominantly oriented toward the practical. But others went on to ponder more deeply the abstract questions, the philosophical and metaphysical presuppositions of the Teaching. The development of philosophical thought was effected under the influence of dogmatic and theological considerations—this much we can learn in spite of the darkness shrouding its history. Later one segment of Mahāyāna scholarship devoted itself with particular zeal to treating the fundamental metaphysical problems without, however, going beyond the limits of orthodoxy (defined rather broadly, to be sure). Walleser, who has studied this problem thoroughly, emphasizes rightly that the original teaching "of course carried within itself the nucleus of further developments, but in and of itself it was still completely indifferent to metaphysical and systematic interpretation."[18] Indeed, this is another instance of the observation made in our first section—so much already exists in potentiality at the beginnings of this wonderful teaching of salvation. If here one thing was drawn forth and another left untouched and there the opposite happened, still a very general direction had been given. The heterogeneity in the development of the individual systems testifies to the broad range given to interpretation.

Significant differences of opinion had already existed in Hīnayāna as, for example, on the nature of the ego. The Pudgalavādin, advocating the teaching of the concrete ego, confronted the Skandhavādin, who opposed the doctrine, while the sequence theories of the Sautrāntika were already approaching views later developed in Mahāyāna. It is not very far from this position to those of the two principal schools of Mahāyāna. In Mādhyamika the elements, which had still been accorded some degree of reality by the "transitoriness" of Sautrāntika, are "nonexistent"; the Vijñānavādin or Yogācārya school developed the theory of Thought-alone out of the doctrine of the dominance of thinking in the ego realm. In compensation, and in order to preserve the authenticity of their interpretation, the Mahāyāna schools expanded the theory of adaptation and the teaching of the manifold truth. The insight into the "voidness" of everything that exists is the quintessence of Mahāyāna philosophy; it is the content of that knowledge which we know to be the highest of the "perfections." It is quiet, stillness—Nirvāṇa. Although it has been called perhaps the most radical "nihilism" that has ever existed, Mādhyamika does away with both affirmation and negation; when both modes of action have been quieted, the spirit enters into perfect stillness.

How can such a philosophy be reconciled with the ethic we have just described? Or with the theology which the ethic presupposes? In order to answer such questions we must remember that the insight into the unreality of everything that exists—even the Buddhas, the beings who belong to them, and the Teaching are illusory—is not intended for everyone. It does not stand at the beginning of the path; rather; the individual can win it only as the fruit of a long, difficult, and tiresome labor, throughout which he believes and hopes as the theology teaches and lives and works as the ethic commands. It is not at all true that the metaphysics of Mahāyāna contradicts its active ethic, as we often read. Rather, the knowledge of which it is comprised is the result of faithful conduct. Such a conception would be deeper than that of Schopenhauer's metaphysics. There "disillusionment" enters the individual existence suddenly and unexpectedly and when, as may happen, it comes at the beginning of that existence, nothing is left to the one who is "saved" but the senseless and aimless vegetating of his only gifts. The same thing is naturally true of Hīnayāna. But Mahāyāna moves the saving knowledge for which it strives out of the present existence and in doing so preserves the possibility of an active ethic. Thus the world, which to the eyes of the Hīnayānist is in a state of the deepest and most hopeless misery, acquires a brighter luster. We are permitted to exercise our disposition toward the good and thus to aspire after that insight which will unveil for us its final, conclusive, and true nature.

As an expression of the outlook on life reflected in these thoughts we should also study the *Saddharma-Puṇḍarīka,* a splendid testimonial to the wisdom of the East.

WILHELM VON HUMBOLDT

TRIBUTE HAS BEEN PAID to a Frenchman and an Englishman as the "two essential liberals" of the nineteenth century. Alexis de Tocqueville and Lord Acton, it was said, "could not be tories or reactionaries or nationalists or rest any authority on mere prescription. . . . They could not, on the other hand, be progressives, doctrinaire equalitarians, or revolutionary socialists," and "they measured all political institutions by the facilities they afforded men to fulfill their moral destinies."

There is a third figure, a German thinker and scholar, philosopher, and statesman, to whom every one of these statements applies: Wilhelm von Humboldt. Of the nobility, as were also de Tocqueville and Lord Acton, he showed himself a true liberal in thought, word, and deed, one deeply con-

NOTE: As noted in the introduction, this article was not printed in Wach's lifetime but was found in his desk after his death. The article is not, perhaps, in the final form Wach would have given it. We print it here, however, because much of Wach's work on nineteenth-century hermeneutics and historiography is unavailable to English readers and because Humboldt's ideas have influenced Wach himself, as those familiar with Wach's other writings will clearly recognize.

cerned with the search for a philosophical or metaphysical basis for the concept of freedom, which is the core of his creed. Like de Tocqueville, the Prussian liberal had an opportunity to serve his country as a minister of state. In the lives of both, however, thought loomed larger than action. There are further parallels: political power which neither de Tocqueville nor Acton sought, was not a temptation to Humboldt, who was a true Hellenist in his belief in the matchless value of genuine *theoria*. In the lives of all three we find something of dash and glamor in the years of youth and the withdrawal to a not uncomfortable inheritance in later life. All three were men of *esprit*, all were passionate correspondents. Just as the admirer of de Tocqueville will cherish his correspondence with Gobineau, so the admirer of Humboldt will value his letters to a friend *(Briefe an eine Freundin)*. Again, traveling played an important role in the life of each one of these three grandseigneurs, yielding lasting fruits in literary works and contributing to the knowledge and understanding of the similarities and differences in human nature. It made all three men true cosmopolitans, though each was proud of and devoted to his country and its culture.

None of the three thinkers was a professional philosopher but each articulated principles that were to govern thought and action. The two Catholics found these principles in their religion, intelligently interpreted, but Humboldt, a Protestant, in whose worldview Hellenism strongly colored Christianity, looked to metaphysics or philosophy for justification. Each of the three scholars was vitally interested in history which each understood as the unfolding of these principles and which each tried to interpret as such. What political life was to de Tocqueville, language was to Humboldt: it was the medium in which he followed the growth and articulation of human freedom. It is hardly an exaggeration to say that no one had ever devoted more profound and more penetrating thought to the nature of speech, to the structure of language, to its psychological and sociological problems, to its typology and its function in the development of human civilization than the sage of Tegel. As the Mezzofanti of his age (Mezzofanti was a polyglot scholar of the eighteenth century, one of the greatest linguists of all times), Humboldt has continued to live in the consciousness of the German people. There was a time when he and his brother Alexander were regarded as the giant "dioscuri" of knowledge, the one holding the keys to the realm of the mind, the other to the realm of nature, yet that period was followed surprisingly soon by an age that "knew not Joseph." The deaths of Goethe, Hegel, Schleiermacher, and Humboldt mark the end of an era. Its heroes were denounced by the generation of the Young Germany of the 1830s and 1840s as aesthetes, cosmopolitans, and quietists. The forces of reaction to which Humboldt had to yield, resigning the hopeless task of liberalizing the Prussian constitution, had been in the ascendancy since the Prussian ruler had begun to prefer Metternich's advice to that of his own liberal advisers. Activism was the answer of the younger liberals. The turbulent period preceding the revolution of 1848 seemed indeed far removed from the "halcyonic quiet between the storms" that prevailed during Humboldt's declining years. The peace which reigned after the revolution had failed was imposed by a reaction to which Humboldt's ideas were as repugnant as those of the revolutionaries. The analogy to the situation in which de Tocqueville found himself after the establishment of the Second Empire is hard to overlook. Later generations remembered the squire of Tegel as the great scholar he had been, eulogized him as the cofounder of the University of Berlin and the father of the humanistic *Gymnasium* but were forgetful or critical of the philosophy for which he had stood. (A biography of Humboldt by Rudolf Haym appeared in 1856.) Neither those imbued with the romantic spirit, a *Weltanschauung* which Humboldt had always regarded with distrust, nor the radical democrats felt that they could learn from him about freedom based on principles. Those in our age who refuse to believe in an alternative between unbridled individualism and egalitarian collectivism will understand him.

There can be no doubt that Humboldt, a friend of Goethe and of Schiller, belongs more to the eighteenth than to the nineteenth century. His philosophy reminds us more of Leibniz than of Herder. His concept of *humanitas,* his belief in the power of reason and in the significance of forms, his view of history and his cosmopolitan outlook separate him from the emerging romantic school. Kant's influence upon his epistemological and moral philosophy is strong. In his aesthetics this influence is balanced by that of the neo-classicists (Winckelmann). Humboldt was a "good European," a designation to which not too many of his compatriots could lay claim. Ernst Troeltsch has shown that it was the romantic movement in Germany and the historicism which it engendered that caused the divergent development in the nineteenth century in Humboldt's country and in England. One cannot but regret that later generations in his homeland did not avail themselves of the precious heritage which Humboldt bequeathed to his nation and did not use the bridges which this philosopher of freedom had constructed over the gulfs that separate the peoples of the civilized world.

Wilhelm von Humboldt, born June 22, 1767, into a Prussian noble family (his father had served as a chamberlain to Frederic the Great), was two years older than his famous brother, Alexander. Predestined to enter the civil service at the earliest opportunity, Wilhelm was given a careful education by liberal-minded teachers. As an attractive and promising young man of means and talent, he was received into the brilliant company of intellectual Berlin. He found himself welcomed into the circle of the aged leaders of the era of Enlightenment (Teller, Moses Mendelssohn) as well as into the intellectual salons in which the budding romantic spirit was cultivated. Two focal points of interest can be discerned at an early date in the young Humboldt's extensive studies. Both subjects, the study of philosophy and the study of antiquity, were to retain their fascination for him until the end of his life. At the age of twenty he entered the University of Frankfurt an-der-Oder but he was soon attracted by the fame of

Göttingen, where the natural sciences and humanities were brilliantly represented. Among his teachers were the great physiologist Blumenbach and the father of modern philology, Heyne, whose successor, F. A. Wolff, the Homeric critic, was to be one of Humboldt's (and incidentally Goethe's) friends and confidants. At this time he pursued his study of Kant, in whose thought he had become interested. Travels around Germany and into Switzerland brought him into contact with the philosophers J. H. Jacobs and Lavater. He married Caroline von Dacheröden, a woman of intelligence and charm, in 1789. A brief period of activity in the civil service did not prove satisfactory to Humboldt. At twenty-four he retired to a family estate in Thuringia to devote himself exclusively to study: "egotist though of the noblest variety, Epicurean if of the finest grain, he took over from destiny which had spoiled him so far, the task of further spoiling," as the historian A. Dove has put it. But the idyll was disturbed by the grave events that shook Europe. The French Revolution made a profound impression upon the mind of the young humanist. Stimulated by a question as to the limits of the jurisdiction of the state, put by Dalberg, the great liberal prince-elector of Mayence, Humboldt wrote down his thoughts on this subject (1791). They were not published until 1851 (translated into English under the title "The Sphere and Duties of Government," 1854) but ever since then they have been regarded as a classical document of liberal German thought. In the following years Humboldt continued to live the life of the gentleman scholar. His philosophical and philological interests centered on studies in the fields of language, criticism, and aesthetics. These studies were stimulated by a close friendship with Schiller, Goethe, and Wolf. The problems of a true education in a humanistic spirit began to loom large in Humboldt's mind *(Gedanken einer Theorie der Menschenbildung)*. Between 1797 and 1808 he traveled extensively in southern Europe. A sojourn in Paris proved as fruitful to his philosophical inclinations as a visit to Spain (the Basque country) for his linguistic aspirations. Meanwhile Humboldt had yielded to the request of his government to lend his services and accepted the post as Prussian envoy to the Vatican (1802–1808). Great changes had occurred when he returned to his homeland, which had been ravished by Napoleon and was more than ever in need of her best sons for the work of reconstruction. Under Schleiermacher's pupil Dohna, Humboldt took over the Department of Education in the Ministry of the Interior. In the short period of his administration he was able to carry through epoch-making reforms in high school and university curricula. To his initiative and planning was due the foundation of the University of Berlin to which Fichte, Hegel, Schleiermacher, Marheineke, Gaus, and others were drawn, as well as the reorganization of the Academy and of the Berlin Museum. The liberal prime minister Count Hardenberg meant to make Humboldt his minister of education but the king vetoed the suggestion on account of the latter's alleged unorthodoxy (Unkirchlichkeit). In 1810 the scholarly diplomat, now recognized as one of the leading liberal statesmen of the New Prussia, accompanied Hardenberg to Vienna. For seven years he took part in the work of the Congress, not without seeking relief from his diplomatic duties in extensive studies in the philosophy of language, which moved more and more to the center of his interests. After a brief period during which he served as envoy to London, Humboldt was appointed minister of the interior to work with Baron von Stein on Prussia's new constitution. But his ideas were for the second time unfavorably received. Difficulties with Hardenberg complicated the situation. On the last day of the year 1819 Humboldt resigned without being granted a pension. This was his final resignation from active service. Once more, withdrawing to the small but beautiful estate of Tegel near Berlin, he turned scholar and hermit and devoted the remaining years of his life almost exclusively to the comparative study of languages. The ancient tongues were but a small though important province in the realm which he explored tirelessly, testing his general theory of linguistic expression by an investigation not only of Indo-European and Semitic idioms but also of Basque and Hungarian, of American Indian languages, of Chinese and South Sea dialects.[1] Visitors found the aged sage "pure and perfect like an ancient work of art."

Widowed in 1829, he followed his great contemporaries Goethe (1832), Hegel (1831) and Schleiermacher (1834) into eternity on March 8, 1835, mourned by his brother Alexander (who was to survive him for nearly a quarter-century), by his nation and by his friends and admirers throughout the civilized world.

The work of Humboldt has been gathered by A. Leitzmann in the fifteen-volume edition of the Prussian Academy (1903ff.). The first of these comprises his essays on religion, on political theory, on the study of antiquity, on education *(Bildung)*, and on anthropology; the second his studies of the eighteenth century and his critical analysis of Goethe's epic *Hermann und Dorothea*. The third includes sketches on Greek civilization, philosophy of history, and travel reports. His epoch-making work on language and languages is found in Volumes 4–5. Early papers are reprinted in Volume 7, while Volume 8 is dedicated to translations, mainly from Greek poetry. Humboldt's poems are gathered in Volume 9, his political writings in Volumes 10–13. The diaries fill the last two tomes of this monumental edition. His correspondence, particularly with his wife, his brother, his friends, and some of the greatest scholars and poets of his age has been separately edited.[2] It is surprising how little has actually been written on Wilhelm von Humboldt and his work. No monograph exists in English. The best German study has been written by a student of the philosopher W. Dilthey, who owes so much to Humboldt: Ed. Spranger's *Wilhelm von Humboldt und die Humanitätsidee* (1909). S. Kaehler's book, *Wilhelm von Humboldt und der Staat* (1929), is an overcritical psychological study and in parts certainly unfair. Most treatises on language and comparative grammar refer to his linguistic work, especially H. Steinthal, and, more recently, E. Cassirer. Humboldt's theory of interpretation (hermeneutics) has been analyzed by this author.

In his critical study of Goethe's poem *Hermann und Dorothea,* Humboldt spoke of the edifice which he planned. Its foundation he found in the education *(Bildung)* of man; the edifice itself was to be the characterization of the human mind *(Gemut)*, its possibilities *(mögliche Anlagen)* in the differences which experience shows us. This formulation expresses Humboldt's double interest in the appearance and the idea of man, a distinction which the philosophy of Kant and Fichte had suggested. If man as he is is the great topic of anthropology and "characterology," disciplines in which Humboldt was passionately interested, then "man as he *should be*" is the topic of ethics and the philosophy of history. Both ideas converge in the concept of education *(Bildung)* which Humboldt defines as "the highest proportional cultivation of the powers of man." This idea is as removed from the ideal of limitless and unqualified self-expression as it is from that of pure intellectual perfection. Humboldt follows Kant, especially his third critique, when he attributes to human imagination the function of establishing unity and harmony between nature and spirit, necessity and contingency, appearance and idea. Such balance he regards as a criterion of true *Bildung*. It is the realization of the purpose for which the individual exists. Humboldt as an empiricist, psychologist, and historian was ever attracted by the riddle of individuality, while his philosophical interest forced him to seek the idea or norm in which reality appears idealized. In art he finds a reconciliation of nature and freedom which reveals itself in the organic character of the work of art. His philosophy of history is focused upon the description of the "endeavor of an idea to incorporate itself in reality." The poet and the historian, he feels, have corresponding tasks. Neither can be satisfied clinging to empirical reality. To both Humboldt assigns the task of strengthening and deepening our sense of "reality" in its ideal aspect, to recognize the true and to conform to it *("das Wahre zu erkennen und sich anzuschliessen")*. Ideas indicate two things: direction and productivity. Individuals and collectives (nations), ages and cultures represent ideas. The task of the philosophical historian is to "portray the highest life" of a people, interpreting the expression of this life symbolically as revealing ideas. Greek civilization is a case in point. "The Greeks," Humboldt states, "are not only a people useful for us to know historically but an ideal." And again: "we manifestly regard antiquity more ideally than it actually was, and we ought to because, by its form and attitude, we are driven to seek therein ideas and effects which transcend life as it surrounds us." The same principle has to guide the critic. In his study of Goethe's epic *Hermann und Dorothea* Humboldt discusses the function of art as idealization by means of the imagination, the concept of artistic objectivity and artistic truth, the difference between classical and modern poetry, and finally, the epic as the genre of *humanitas (Humanität)*. The study of history as well as that of literature broadens our understanding of mankind *(Menschheit)* in enabling us to transcend the limitations of our own empirical individuality. To understand man means to know his various abilities *(Kräfte)*, their modifications, their relation to each other and to external circumstances. In other words, it means to find the rules of the transformation which is effected with necessity from within and according to possibilities from without. The more vital notions of human experiences we have acquired by this study, the more transformations the soul is enabled to achieve.

How does one acquire this knowledge? How do we learn to understand men and nations, the destinies of individuals or of culture? Humboldt answers that we have to react with our total being *("mit vereinten Kräften")* and that we have to assimilate ourselves to what we desire to comprehend *("ähnlich machen")*. He is aware of the unending character of this task. Not all manifestations of human activity and thought, however, are equally valuable and important. We are confronted with a circle in Humboldt's reasoning: the truly representative, the truly "human" expressions should be valued most highly. These truly "human" expressions the great student of antiquity considers to be those of the Greeks. (See especially his essay on *Latinum und Hellas*, containing his philosophy, as it were, *in nuce.)* There are typical peoples and individuals, as there are unique ones. The "typical" may be negatively explained as a lack of individuality or as elementary simplicity. There may be variety and unity in one character while in another multiplicity prevails. Humboldt can be regarded as one of the founders of the modern theory of types which plays such an important part in contemporary psychology and sociology (Dilthey, Spranger, Max Weber).

In his essay on the eighteenth century, originally conceived as part of a comprehensive anthropological and psychological work which he never completed, Humboldt articulated methodological principles for studying that era as any other. All single features are to be compressed under a few separate, salient points, into a figure; each degree and modification of the contributing forces is to be viewed as part of an infinite quantity. While it would be unnecessary to aspire to completeness, it would be insufficient merely to indicate the outlines of the phenomenon. Its spirit, its character, must be caught; if it is captured, no stroke of the brush needs to be added. The gathering of the data is the function of the observing intellect, while imagination organizes them into a balanced whole. Neither agreement with "reality" nor inner consistency is, in this theory, the test of the truth and the adequacy of the resulting picture; the criterion is its efficacy in stimulating and directing the power of our imagination. This is possible only if the image is true and "alive." If it proves such it will produce the widening, determining, and orienting effect which we call education *(Bildung)*. Humboldt felt that the study of human character types had been neglected: neither the deductive reasoning of the philosophers nor practical moral treatises had done them justice. The poets were the only exception. (Dilthey, who refers to Humboldt frequently in his writings, says as much in his *Contributions to the Study of Individuality.*) "Character" can be defined as the permanent form of unity in changeable matter. To grasp it, the peculiar or unique, that which distinguishes one person from another, has to be found. It is here designated as the degree of inner power. The relation and the movements of these inner forces determine, according to him, the differences of character. The characterologist must ascertain the dominating power, a concept that reminds us of Leibniz's *vinculum substantiale.* A dynamic concept of the relation of the inner forces permits the understanding of the development of a character. The result will not be abstract notions but an appeal to the imagination to help it reproduce the integrated picture of a character. As other masters of hermeneutics have done,

Humboldt postulates a circle—though not of the vicious variety: only through the empirical observation of manifestations and expressions can we arrive at an understanding of the inner forces that determine a character, but we need to understand these inner forces to interpret the manifestation correctly. The close interrelationship of body and mind cannot be overlooked. It is necessary to distinguish between accidental and essential elements in the structure of a character, relative as such distinctions will be.

Rarely will a character express itself in full purity. Certain features may appear exaggerated. Summary characterizations are based on exaggerated features, such as the statement that women are weak or Frenchmen are witty. Humboldt devoted two essays to the characterology of the sexes, a problem that greatly intrigued his romantic contemporaries. He holds that not all forces in nature can work simultaneously but that the secret of nature consists in reciprocal interaction. Form and matter affect each other: nothing is purely active or passive. Differentiation according to sexes should be seen in this light. The productive force is meant more for action (the male principle), while the receptive force is destined for reaction. All acting is bound to matter upon which it acts. The most independent spirit is also the most irritable; the most receptive heart reciprocates with the liveliest energy. The initial direction is determinative. Virility is life force maximally deprived of matter. Femininity is longing for the awakening of the fullness of matter. Masculinity is directed outward; femininity, inward. To the male form corresponds intellect, to the female, feeling. However, these potentials are nowhere found pure: individuality limits and transforms them. A "pure" human being does not exist. But in ideal beauty the regularity of form is manifested as the free play of matter. The origin of the two less perfect sexes means a disturbance of the balance though not an ending of the connection of the two forces. According to Humboldt the sexes approximate each other: each is a general expression of humankind. Sex is a limitation. The characteristically human must ennoble the character of sex. Sex is to be interpreted as the road to the perfection of humankind, that is, the balancing of the natural by the moral element. The philosopher sees a new beauty arising out of this union of humanity and sex, an intermediate beauty in which the balance of the male and the female is achieved. Man appears more energetic, woman softer than the sexless being would be. Upon his metaphysics of sex Humboldt develops his theory of genius, a theme to which the philosophers and artists of the eighteenth century had given so much thought and which looms large in the aesthetics of idealist and romantic thinkers alike. Genius can be defined as spiritual productivity. Each work of genius kindles the enthusiasm for a new one, thus effecting procreation. It actually consists in the union and interaction of activity and receptivity. The genius goes beyond the empirical and delves into the self that is "necessary," thus transforming his subjective existence into one of the highest objectivity. The creative mood can be described as a gathering of force, a feeling of strength, but also of longing for what, once a union is consummated, will make for wholeness and completion. Just as the most intense energy of the male and the most enduring persistence of the female principle form the unlimited power of nature, as love and life consist in separating and uniting, in restlessness and steadiness, in energy and being, so the creative and the receptive forces work to produce the perfect creation of genius: the more matter is formed by the creative force, the more intense the struggle, the greater the effect. Everything limited, according to Humboldt, is liable to destruction, "heavenly peace dwells alone in the realm of that which is sufficient in itself."

None of the categories that can be devised to help us understand the individual will ultimately do justice to it. That is Humboldt's conviction, and he never tires of reiterating it. In the "secret of individuality" we find the essence and destiny of human nature. "Within the boundaries of earthly existence we cannot expect a true revelation of the secret of individuality." It goes without saying that all attempts to explain it by studying the circumstances under which the true ego, the individual personality, emerges would have been rejected by this defender of freedom.

Because he viewed the odyssey of humanity as the endless attempt to achieve its idea in the individual, Humboldt could define the task of its interpreter, the philosopher-historian, as "the delineation of the striving of an idea to come into existence." This program is formulated in a classical lecture on "The Task of the Historian." Its execution is found in Humboldt's greatest single enterprise, *Linguistic Variability and Intellectual Development*. This essay remains, according to Daniel Brinton, the most suggestive work written on the philosophy of language. Conceived as the introduction to an analysis of the Kawi language of Java, this book actually is the ripest fruit of the great linguist's interest in human speech and its products, an interest that lasted throughout his life. Humboldt devoted at least three major treatises to the comparative study of language and languages, not counting his numerous studies of ancient dialects and literatures. The close relationship between empirical inquiry and generalizing theory characteristic of Wilhelm von Humboldt's methodology prevails throughout his linguistic studies. With all the fascination that detail could exert upon his scholarly mind, the author never appears overwhelmed by it. "The foundation of all linguistic study remains the philosophical view, and at every point, however concrete, one has to be ever conscious of its relation to the general and necessary features." Humboldt states in his monograph on the dual that, though the study of language should be pursued for its own sake, it "resembles other branches of learning in not having its ultimate purpose in itself but that it conforms to the general purpose of interest in the human mind to help humanity to realize its true nature and its relation to everything visible and invisible around and above itself."

The most important task of the study of language is formulated by Humboldt in a treatise on the languages of the South Seas, as "the endeavor to investigate the differences in the structure of human speech, to describe them in their essential conditions, to lucidly organize the apparently infinite variety from well chosen points of view, to examine the sources of their structural diversity and their influence upon the thought, perception, and feeling of the speakers, finally to follow through all transformations of history the mental development of humanity, guided by that profoundly revealing expression: language."

In harmony with his general philosophical principles Humboldt regards language, the single word as well as connected speech, as an act, "a truly creative act of the mind." Speech can be defined as the forming organ of thought by which the activity of the intellect becomes externalized and perceptible and the process of thinking is completed. The great linguist stresses the creative nature of speech. Language is the ever-recurring effort of the mind to express thought. Language, however, he insists, does not manifest itself in an abstract form; it appears always broken by the media of nationality and individuality. Thus it undergoes deep modifications, or better, it takes on its character by the process of articulation to which the spirit of the nation or the individual subjects it. Thus Humboldt can regard language as the outward manifestation of the mind of the peoples who create it; their language "is" their mind and their mind "is" their language. The character of a language he sees hinging on the smallest details.

A language consists of two constituents: it sounds and its capacity for articulation. To the former element Humboldt attributes the differences in human speech, the latter he is inclined to regard as universal. In the nature of sound he finds the true individuality of a language, each people showing, in its system of sounds, its unique preferences. The distinguishing character of a language is produced by the use of a system of sounds and by their articulation through the faculty that Humboldt calls *Sprachsinn*. This distinguishing character he designated in a famous phrase as *Innere Sprachform* (interior form). As form and matter are balanced in a perfect work of art, so both elements of linguistic expression are in perfect proportion in a fully developed language, none prevailing over the other. Hence language can be defined as "the ever repeated activity of the mind, fashioning the articulated sound as a vehicle for thoughts." By giving expression to thought through the lips, the product, according to Humboldt's theory, returns to the ear. In this way language divides and fosters the inner nature of thought. In the world of appearance, language is always social; man can only understand himself in trying out his words tentatively on others. However, Humboldt is of the opinion that speech is a necessary condition of the thinking even of the isolated individual in his solitude. This master of linguistic analysis is the first to lay the foundation of a sociology of language, an achievement not commonly recognized. He holds that speaking and understanding are to be regarded as effects of the capacity of expression. Mental communication always presupposes that something exists in common between the two who exchange it: one understands what one hears, only because one could have said it (potentially). Language is actually mine because I produce it, says Humboldt, but he adds that the power of the individual is small. All linguistic change is gradual: its extent, rapidity, and the nature of its transformations depend upon the liveliness of exchange and the degree of depth with which the language is grasped. No language remains the same, according to Humboldt, even through a decade or in any extensive territory. An interesting sociological problem which he was the first to raise is that of the specialized languages of women in some civilizations, of certain professions and classes, the poetic and court idioms, etcetera. The difference, he suggests, may either be lexical or pertain to the grammatical structure.

In his analysis of the methods by which words in different languages are connected to make sentences Humboldt arrives at his famous typology of isolation, agglutination, incorporation, and inflection, illustrated in Chinese, Turkish, the Mexican language, and Sanskrit. These differences point to a different degree of formative power, that is, of the capacity to utilize sounds for the expression of thought. Not what can be expressed in a language but its capacity to quicken and stimulate mental action determines its superiority or deficiency, the criterion being the clarity, definiteness, and mobility of the ideas that the language evokes in the nation whose spirit has created it and upon which it in turn reacts. The ideal is the accurate correspondence between structure and sound and the topical procedure of thought.

Peoples and nations differ as to the energy of thought they bring to bear upon the vocal material at their disposal for the expression of ideas. They differ also in the degree of understanding of which they are capable. The more they are able to sense and to be moved by what Humboldt calls *das Menschliche,* the greater will be their capacity to comprehend and to interpret human existence, past and present. All the variety which a comparative study of language as the organ of the inner life of a people reveals to us must be understood as the variegated manifestation of the human mind, the highest of all possible ideas. We will grasp this idea if we know how to blend the understanding of the individual and the manifold with that of the eternally human. In order to understand man and his creation in artistic and linguistic expression, our organs of comprehension must be activated. They are perfected in and by the exercise of this power of comprehension.

SOCIOLOGY OF RELIGION

The Nature and Aims of a Sociology of Religion

Like other sociological disciplines—the sociology of art or of law—the sociology of religion is the offspring of two different scholarly pursuits, the study of society and the study of religion.[1] Its character, methods, and aims reflect this parentage. In addition to the problems which the sociology of religion inherits from the two parental disciplines, it has its own peculiar difficulties and tasks. That is to say, sociology of religion shares with the sociology of other activities of man certain problems and, in addition, has its own due to the peculiar nature of religious experience and its expression. (The theory of religious experience is to be worked out by the philosopher, theologian, and psychologist in cooperation with the student of religion.)

The sociology of religion is a young branch of study, not more than half a century old. That does not mean that major contributions toward an inquiry into the nature of socioreligious phenomena were not made long before, but as an organized systematic discipline (emancipated from the older disciplines in and from which it developed) the sociology of religion is of recent date. Earlier contributions were made by students in widely different fields: theology, philosophy, philology, jurisprudence and the social sciences, and later archeology and anthropology. A great deal of material was thus gathered, particularly in the course of the nineteenth century, and periodically grouped and reviewed from theological and philosophical, psychological and sociological viewpoints. What was lacking, at least until the beginning of the twentieth century, finally evolved through the cooperation of a group of outstanding scholars of different nationalities: *categories* with which to organize the vast material assembled. The sociology of religion had to develop its own methodology based on an unbiased examination of the nature of its subject matter.

Before we can survey attempts in this direction we have to trace briefly some of the major trends in the development of studies to be integrated into a systematic sociology of religion. It is perhaps significant that the exchange of ideas and mutual interdependence between the scholars of various nations—American, English, Dutch, French, German, Scandinavian—in this discipline has been as strong as, if not stronger than, in other fields of sociological research.

I

THE EMERGENCE OF A SOCIOLOGY OF RELIGION BY COOPERATIVE INTERNATIONAL EFFORTS OF DIFFERENT SCHOOLS

THE FRENCH SOCIOLOGY OF RELIGION

The French sociology of religion was characterized all through the nineteenth century by the dominance of the tenets of the philosophy of history as sociology, as developed by Auguste Comte and his successors.[2] Its course, methodology, and aims were determined by students of sociology, not by those of religion. It was conceived in a broad, encyclopedic attempt to review the life and growth of society; it was determined by the interest in an application of "scientific" methods ("laws") to sociohistorical phenomena including religious ideas and institutions (theory of stages of development), and finally by the endeavor to include the material gathered in anthropological and ethnological research. Theological and metaphysical norms were to be replaced by positivistic principles. That is, positive philosophy was to set the norms for the organization of life and society. According to this conception, mankind is not only the subject but also the object of religion.

The first trend of modern French sociology of religion is marked by the well-known works of Emile Durkheim[3] and other contemporary writers: Lucien Lévy-Bruhl, Marcel Mauss, and so forth. Durkheim's concept of sociology is characterized by a marked emancipation from the tenets of Comte's philosophy of history as sociology (sociology as a method) and by a corresponding tendency toward construction of a typology of social groupings, in which he included religious communities. In his concept of the nature of religion he agrees with Comte. His chef d'oeuvre, *Les formes élémentaires de la vie religieuse,* applies the categories of a typological sociology to the data of primitive religious communities. Lévy-Bruhl concentrates his attention upon the psychological investigation of group consciousness in primitive society.[4] *L'Année sociologique* for over a decade formed the center of studies in the sociology of religion.

A second trend is indicated by the synthetic studies of a number of French scholars such as Numa Denis Fustel de Coulanges and E. F. A. Count Goblet d'Alviella, and more recently Arnold Van Gennep and Paul Foucart.[5] In their writings certain concepts, rites, and institutions fundamental to religious group life are analyzed and compared. Inasmuch as these authors did not limit themselves to a discussion of primitive society, though they did concentrate on non-Christian religions, a rapprochement between sociological and sociopsychological studies, on the one hand, and the efforts of the school of "comparative religions" (F. Max Mueller, C. P. Tiele, W. Robertson Smith), on the other, was effected. The latter investigations were carried on by a school of students of religion who aspired to emancipation from theological conceptions, working for the establishment of a science of religion on the basis of the critical (historical and philological) and comparative methods.

The third trend is characterized by (1) a clearer methodological consciousness concerning the field, purpose, and method of the sociology of religion; (2) a profounder understanding of the nature of religious communion; (3) a rapprochement between students of religion from theological and philosophical points of view, and of students of society.[6] Outstanding are the works of Raoul de la Grasserie and H. Pinard de la Boullaye, S. J., of Roger Bastide and Robert Will. The last phase reflects to a considerable extent the influence of the German sociology of religion of Max Weber and Ernst Troeltsch (particularly the studies of Robert Will).

To Pinard de la Boullaye we owe the best existing history of the study of religion and a thorough discussion of its methods, including the sociological approach. He gives attention to the social organization of religion and to the problem of authority. The work of de la Grasserie is more important than is often realized. It is characterized by a keen systematic interest, by relative absence of the preconceptions of the positivistic school, and by comprehensiveness of material. Though he presses the analogy of the religious body with the physical organism and though his concept of the "divine society" is open to criticism, de la Grasserie does offer helpful categories for the understanding of "external religious society," and particularly of the "societies to the second power," as created by prophets and saints. The relations between religious and civil societies receive his attention. Bastide's brief summary extends the field of the sociology of religion too widely; only one chapter ("L'organisation religieuse") deals with its tasks as we will have to define it. The most comprehensive treatment of the subject in French is now Robert Will's volumes on the nature and forms of cults with which this author, who was familiar with Will's outline in German, agrees on many important points. The study makes the three-fold assumption that man, in his cultic functions, faces God, the world of cultic forms, and the religious community. It presents first an analysis of man's communion with God ("communion in God"), including a review of the main types of cultic activity (sacrifice, mystery, prayer) and of religious attitudes (mystery and revelation on the divine side, adoration and edification on the human side). Second, it offers an inquiry into the principles (causes, laws, values), the forms (media, personnel, action, and atmosphere), and finally the general sociological categories of religious communality, in virtual if not conscious agreement with the theories of Scheler, Litt, and Mead. This exposition is followed by an analysis of the cultic group and its milieu and symbols. Lack of space precludes a detailed discussion of Will's system in this context.

GERMAN SOCIOLOGY OF RELIGION

(a) *Philosophical* preoccupation with the various types of cultural activities on an idealistic basis (Johann Gottfried Herder, G. W. F. Hegel, Johann Gustav Droysen, Hermann Steinthal, Wilhelm Wundt); (b) *legal studies* (Aemilius Ludwig, Richter, Rudolf Sohm, Otto Gierke); (c) *philology and archeology*, both stimulated by the romantic movement of the first decades of the nineteenth century; (d) *economic theory and history* (Karl Marx, Lorenz von Stein, Heinrich von Treitschke, Wilhelm Roscher, Adolf Wagner, Gustav Schmoller, Ferdinand Tönnies); (e) *ethnological research* (Friedrich Ratzel, Adolf Bastian, Rudolf Steinmetz, Johann Jakob Bachofen, Hermann Steinthal, Richard Thurnwald, Alfred Vierkandt, P. Wilhelm Schmidt), on the one hand; and historical and systematical work in *theology* (church history, canonical law—*Kirchenrecht*), systematic theology (Schleiermacher, Richard Rothe), and *philosophy of religion*, on the other, prepared the way during the nineteenth century for the following era to define the task of a sociology of religion and to organize the material gathered by these pursuits.[7] The names of Max Weber, Ernst Troeltsch, Werner

Sombart, and Georg Simmel—all students of the above-mentioned older scholars—stand out. Weber fostered more than anybody else the investigation of the relation between economics and society, on the one hand, and religion, on the other—typologically and historically in *Gesammelte Aufsätze zur Religionssoziologie* and systematically in *Wirtschaft und Gesellschaft*. Troeltsch, concentrating on the Christian world, presented his comprehensive studies of Christian groups and their social and moral concepts *(Soziallehren der christlichen Kirchen)*. To Sombart we owe extensive treatment of the development of forms of economical and correlative social and religious concepts.[8] In Georg Simmel's *Soziologie* the first consistent attempt at a purely formal sociology was made; in his sociology of religion Simmel follows Durkheim.[9] After World War I a new generation of sociologists (Karl Dunkmann, Leopold von Wiese,[10] Alfred Vierkandt, Ottmar Spann) and of students of religion, both Protestant and Catholic (Romano Guardini, G. Gundlach, Johann Baptist Kraus)—the most outstanding of which was Max Scheler[11]—followed the lead of the older generation (cf. "Erinnerungsgabe für Max Weber"), joined by Scandinavian and Dutch scholars (especially Gerardus van der Leeuw, whose work is one of the most important contributions to the comparative study of religions between the two wars, and Hendrik Kraemer). The philosophical and historical work of Wilhem Dilthey, himself averse to establishing an independent sociological discipline, proved to be important systematically and epistemologically (Theodor Litt, Joachim Wach).[12]

With the advent of National Socialism the official philosophical and racial teachings of the Third Reich, prepared by its ideological forerunners, began to make themselves felt in all disciplines concerned with the study of religion and of society. (Cf. the later volumes of the *Archiv für Religionswissenschaft*). No significant contribution in our field can be listed.[13]

ENGLISH SOCIOLOGY OF RELIGION

In England the development of legal and historical studies (Henry Sumner Maine, Frederic William Maitland, Paul Vinogradoff, Ernest Barker) coalesced with anthropological (Edward Burnett Tylor, John Lubbock, Andrew Lang, James George Frazer) and psychological research (Robert Ranulph Marett, Graham Wallace, A. R. Radcliffe-Brown).[14] In philosophy the empirical and naturalistic school (John Stuart Mill, Herbert Spencer) as well as the idealistic (Thomas Hill Green, Bernard Bosanquet) focused their attention on the problems of the nature and development of society. The concept of evolution (Charles Darwin, Herbert Spencer, Walter Begehot, Edward Westermarck) and the methodology of positivism (Thomas Buckle) had far-reaching influence. Though the task of a sociology of religion has never been as clearly and systematically defined as in France and Germany, great contributions were made in England through the cooperation of the students of the gradually emerging sociology (Leonard T. Hobhouse, Morris Ginsberg, Robert M. MacIver) and of the study of history (Charles H. MacIlvain and John N. Figgis) and of economics (C. C. J. Webb, Richard Tawney) with students of religion interested in the problems of social theology. Anglican and Nonconformist theologians, philosophers, and writers (Thomas Carlyle, John Ruskin, Frederic Dennis Maurice, Charles Kingsley), especially the Christian Socialists, were interested in the normative aspect of the problems of religion and society.[15] In the younger generation several of these trends are blended: William Temple, John MacMurray, Maurice B. Rickett, Vigo A. Demant.[16] Max Weber's influence in England never reached as deep as in France or the United States; it remained limited to his theories on economics. On the other hand, the studies in "comparative religion," stimulated by the untiring efforts of Max Mueller, were cultivated at Oxford and Cambridge in close contact with continental archeological, philological, and historical investigations (Ernest Crawley, Gilbert Murray, Jane Harrison, Frank Byron Jevons, E. O. James).[17]

NORTH AMERICAN SOCIOLOGY OF RELIGION[18]

In the United States interest in the sociology of religion was stimulated by the encyclopedic tendencies of the earlier sociologists (William Graham Sumner, Albert G. Keller, Edward A. Ross)[19] and by the work of historical and systematical social theology (Francis G. Peabody, Charles A. Ellwood, Shailer Mathews, Shirley J. Case). The movement of the Social Gospel focused the attention of students of religion on social phenomena from a normative point of view.[20] The peculiar problems of American denominationalism (Heinrich H. Maurer, H. Richard Niebuhr, William Warren Sweet, Paul Douglass)[21] are reflected in the interest in socioreligious statistics (William F. Ogburn) and urban-rural studies (Robert E. Park, Ernest W. Burgess, Carle C. Zimmerman and H. P. Douglass, Edward de S. Brunner, John H. Kolb).[22] Catholic scholars have shown their interest by critical and positive investigations supplemented by philosophical reflection.[23] Cultural anthropology, experiencing an unprecedented development in the United States, contributed immense and valuable material on ideas, customs, and institutions of primitive peoples, and, to a considerable extent, categories with which to order it (Daniel Brinton, Franz Boas, Alfred Kroeber, Clark Wissler, Paul Radin, Bronislaw Malinowski, Robert H. Lowie, Ralph Linton).[24] Social psychology began to form a bridge between sociological and psychological studies (James Mark Baldwin, Wm. McDougall, R. E. Park, George H. Mead, Ellsworth Faris, Charles A. Ellwood).[25] Philosophical (John Dewey, George H. Mead, Olaf Boodin, William E. Hocking, Edgar Brightman)[26] and sociological theory and analysis (Mark Baldwin, Charles H. Cooley, Ellsworth Faris, R. M. MacIver, Howard Becker, Talcott Parsons) prepared the way for an understanding of socioreligious organization, while detailed sociological analysis of relevant phenomena[27] was carried on by William I. Thomas, Florian Znaniecki, M. E. Gaddis, Arthur E. Holt, Samuel Kincheloe, W. Lloyd Warner, and others.[28] Max Weber's influence is felt in the synthetic studies of William F. Albright (*From Stone Age to Monotheism*).[29] A systematic treatment of the problems of the sociology of religion has been undertaken more recently with broad perspective by Pitirim Sorokin and, influenced by Weber, Troeltsch, and Dilthey, by Joachim Wach.

SOCIOLOGY OF RELIGION AND ALLIED FIELDS

As with other fields of sociological research the question has been asked if there is good enough reason to treat socioreligious phenomena separately instead of handling them in the traditional disciplines (theology, philosophy, anthropology, etcetera).[30] Yet, as against such doubts, the work done by modern scholarship has proved the right to an independent existence of "sociology of religion." The interdependence of this branch of studies with others, however, is not only historically conditioned but has its raison d'être in the nature of its subject matter. There has been much discussion whether the sociologist of religion is right in viewing his material from a special point of view and handling it according to a special method, or whether he has a more or less well-circumscribed field which he can call his own. The first concept seems to lead to unending controversy, and it is indeed doubtful if the application of just a viewpoint or method could justify the setting up of a separate discipline of studies. Though the sociologist of religion makes use of a specific method—paralleled by that employed in other branches of applied sociology—he is in the position to claim a distinct group of phenomena as his own. Although religious group life, the very subject he attempts to study, can also be examined from theological and juridical viewpoints, it can be shown that when the work of all these disciplines is accomplished, there still remains a task to be done.

II

CONTROVERSIAL ISSUES AND CRITICISM

In the definition of aims, methods and limits of the new discipline there is still, in spite of growing unification and concentration, disagreement on a number of major points.

NORMS

Opinion is divided as to whether sociology of religion should be a normative or descriptive science, and, if the latter, to what extent sociology of religion can and ought to be descriptive. Historically, sociology of religion—as general sociology—originated from both the growing social consciousness in the wake of the industrial development in the modern western world and of its social consequences, and the failure of the official academic philosophy and theology to take this development into account. The situation in Catholicism differed from that in Protestantism. So it is not surprising that considerable confusion prevailed at first, which was partly due to terminological difficulties and partly to a dissensus on the question of aim and method. As sociology came to mean a weapon of aggression for some, others, bent on the defensive, wanted a "religious," "Christian," or "Protestant" sociology. They all agreed that the aim of sociology of religion was to establish norms. As previously indicated, it took considerable time for the development of the concept of a descriptive sociology of religion, implying that the establishment of norms was the concern of the theologian, philosopher, and social theoretician. In the meantime, the newly emerging discipline was suspected by many—and not without reason—to be guided by ulterior motives and by intentions hostile or a least indifferent to religious claims. This problem will be discussed below. Even among scholars who conceive of the study of the interrelation of religion and society as primarily a descriptive task, there are quite a few who do not deny the normative interest which ultimately (originally and finally) dictates the inquiry. But they feel that in order to make the results more than subjective impressions, preferences, or evaluations, chances for verification of the results must be given. That implies abstinence—at least methodical—and temporal—from all subjective evaluation and the use of all the methodological and critical tools which have been developed in the humanities in the course of the nineteenth century. Yet they would feel not justified in regarding their result as the last word of wisdom but would very definitely expect an appreciation and evaluation which puts these results in the proper perspective of a unified system of knowledge, philosophy, or theology; and it is irrelevant whether the latter task is performed in personal union with that of description so long as the integrity of the latter is guaranteed. The question is not so much whether it is possible, justifiable, or advisable to have a viewpoint or standpoint from which to pass such judgment but rather where the proper place for introducing it ought to be.

As long as the topics to be dealt with are removed from the investigator's immediate interest and concern, the difficulties seem to be not so great. There is no reason why a Roman Catholic, a Protestant, and, say, a Marxist student should not concur in their study of American Indian ceremonial, Babylonian mythology, or Buddhist ethics. But the difficulties are greater if the topic were the causes of the Reformation or the nature of the sect. Yet we like to believe that, though there is a Catholic and a Marxian philosophy of society, there can be only *one* sociology of religion which we may approach from different angles and realize to a different degree but which would use but one set of criteria. Divergence of opinion is caused not so much by the variety and difference of the views on society as by those on religion. Though it seems by no means necessary to have identical concepts of the nature and function of religion, it is desirable not to be determined by antipathy or sympathy to the degree which would make an objective investigation impossible. Objectivity does not presuppose indifference, just as sympathy or antipathy does not necessarily disqualify one for an unbiased examination according to the historical or critical method. Once the possibility of understanding a religion different from our own in time and space is admitted, there is no reason why the student can not try to apply the principles of investigation in all instances.

COMPARISON

A few words might be said about the role of the *comparative* method in the study of socio-religious phenomena. In the second half of the nineteenth century the importance of comparison as a help to the understanding of the subject of humanistic studies became recognized. The science of religion was no exception. For a while the unlucky term "comparative religion" (for comparative study of religion) was extremely popular. Everything was compared to everything else, superficial similarity passing frequently for identity. Now there can be no doubt that analogies can be very helpful for the interpretation not only of religious concepts and rites, but also of forms of religious organization. Yet it must be understood that individual features have to be interpreted as part of the configuration they form and that it is dangerous to isolate them from the context in which they occur.

MEANING

This leads us to another methodological problem which we have had occasion to touch upon previously. The hermeneutical principle of understanding configurations as meaningful wholes warrants a further conclusion. Religious ideas, rites, and forms of organization have a *meaning* to which the sociologist of religion has to do justice, just as has the historian or psychologist of religion. In other words, concepts like *Communion of Saints, Familia Dei,* etc. want to be understood with their full *intention.* We will realize it in paying attention to the interpretation which is given these terms in the group which acknowledges them. This realization does by no means imply assent, for the normative quest is excluded; rather it enables the interpreter to understand the phenomenon in the context in which it belongs. The sociologist of religion must give his most serious consideration to the *self-interpretation* of any religious group he studies.

VALUE AND VALIDITY

We come now to one of the most difficult and delicate problems of the methodology of our field which has caused a great deal of discussion and misunderstanding. The failure to find an adequate solution has more than anything else prevented for a long time a fruitful cooperation between students of sociology and of religion. (There is little comfort in the observation that a very similar situation prevails in the relation of psychology to the science of religion).

It is understandable that the idealistic emphasis on the efficacy of spiritual motives and forces, ideas, and energies in the philosophy and history of the early nineteenth century led to a reaction which urged students of social life and development to concentrate on the opposite viewpoint according to which spiritual developments have to be regarded as products of material conditions (Feuerbach, Marx, Engels, against Hegel). There was definitely some justification for correcting a one-sided interpretation of the social "roots" and conditions out of which in the history of man religious concepts and institutions have grown and are growing. The mistake begins when this relation is interpreted in deterministic terms and when the conclusion is drawn that a statement on the (social) origins and conditions of an idea or phenomenon means or implies an answer to the question of its value or validity. It continues and gets worse when the reverse, the shaping of social factors, conditions, and orders by spiritual (religious) forces is overlooked or denied, as we find it in a legion of modern studies more or less dedicated to economic determinism.

The crucial term which is of the greatest importance in this context is "ideology." What is meant by designating certain religious concepts of a cult group ("brotherhood," "communion of saints") as "ideology"? The Marxian understanding is that they are, thus labeled, "debunked," shorn of any claim to validity, that they are, psychologically speaking, illusions. Others would not go so far but feel inclined to interpret ideologies as ideas originated from and hence in their validity limited to a certain sociological sphere. Max Scheler, the creator of the modern "sociology of knowledge," has coined the term relationism—as distinct from relativism—for this theory. It certainly will appeal more than the former interpretation to anyone who identifies himself, traditionally or on his own decision, with any one religious value or a system of religious values. Yet this theory seems also to conflict with the claims of universal validity which are characteristic certainly not of all but of a great part of religious messages, interpretations, and systems. This contradiction is, however, more apparent than real. Does the teaching of an Isaiah or a Luther, even if "explained" sociologically, really lose any of its validity? It does not seem so. Even if it could be shown that economic or general social conditions in a given society have prompted a desire for deliverance, the ideas of redemption that may be included in a religious message are not invalidated by an inquiry into their social "background," provided we do not conceive of the relation in deterministic terms but consider conditions as a framework which may include a variety of contents. We feel that an understanding of the origins, the development, and the meaning of the teachings, practices, and organization of a religious group to which the sociologist of religion tries to contribute, would not only not interfere with but would actually intensify the loyalty of the members of the group. Once the suspicion is removed that the sociologist has an axe to grind and that he is bent on demonstrating the illusionary character of religious ideas and concepts when inquiring into their sociological background, the cooperation of science of religion and sociology of religion will be more fruitful. The interpretation of the meaning of concepts, acts, and behavior given by devout individuals or groups may or may not agree with the findings of the historian, psychologist, or sociologist. The members of a group may deceive themselves as to the primary motives prompting them to think, act, or feel as they do. The case is simple where the ideological, philosophical, or theological justification for a type of rule (e.g.) is a front behind which lust for domination and ambition for power hide. Here the official ideology and the actual state of things obviously do not coincide. But the problem is frequently much more difficult, as psychologists (Jung) and social philosophers (Nietzsche, Sorel, Pareto, Spengler) have shown that the analysis of the social conditioning of ideas and convictions, though in itself not entitling to decisions as to their validity or invalidity, may contribute to the realization of the partial character of views or intentions expressed in them. "The function of the findings of sociology of knowledge lies somewhere in a fashion hitherto not clearly understood, between irrelevance to the establishment of truth on the one hand, and entire adequacy for determining truth on the other."[31] The idea of the particularization of the validity of expressions of religious experience will have to be followed out in epistemology and in the theory of religious experience.

EMPIRICISM VS. APRIORISM

Another point on which opinions are divided is the question of which of two approaches should be used by the sociologist of religion, the *empirical* or the *aprioristic*. One group of scholars advocates the first, gathering data without regard to any scheme or any preconceived idea of the phenomenon in question. An extreme example is the statistical school. The other extreme is represented by students who like to start with a given, "intuited," or deduced concept of, for example, the nature of prayer and sacrifice or of sin and grace. It is easy to see that we are here not really confronted with an alternative because the empiricist can not wholly dispense with categories with which to organize his facts, nor can his opponent forego documentation and illustration of ideas by empirical (historical) facts. Flesh and bones—both are indispensible, neither an unorganized mass nor a mere skeleton would be satisfactory. The typological method, which has been advocated by a number of sociologists of religion, serves the function of bridging the gap between the two extremes: the richer and finer it is developed the more it will serve to combine wealth of detailed information with keen structural analysis.

INDIVIDUALISM VS. COLLECTIVISM

A disagreement exists also between the advocates of an *individualistic* and those of a *collectivistic* view of society and of religion. More than in the case of the previously mentioned alternatives, questions of principles are involved here. While some are inclined to view the process of civilization and of religious growth as a progressive realization of the infinite value of the individual, others are inclined to give priority to the whole before its parts and to consider as central in religion acts constituted by communal worship. Again we are not really faced by an alternative. The sociologist of religion will realize that it is rather a question of emphasis; individual expression and pecularity being present already on the level of so-called primitive civilization and communal worship playing a most important part in the highest forms of religion and culture.

IDENTITY OF INFLUENCE

In anthropology, one of the neighboring sciences, a long controversy developed between the advocates of seemingly alternative attempts to explain *similarities* of thought and behaviour patterns in less advanced cultures and societies. One school—both sides are represented in each, French, English, German and American research—is inclined to interpret all such similarities as the result of historical influences. The other sees in them the indication of an identical constitution and endowment of man. Inasmuch as the sociologist of religion is confronted with the necessity of accounting for apparently identical or similar patterns in religious behavior, ideas, and forms of organizations on different cultural levels, he is interested in a constructive solution of the apparent dilemma. Observation and reflection, however, will tell him that he is not faced with a true alternative. He will distrust all hasty assumption of equality as long as there is a change of historical derivation from other sources while not refusing to allow for independent growth and development of religious concepts and institutions under analogous conditions and circumstances. (Not enough attention has been paid to Rudolf Otto's paper "Das Gesetz der Parallelen in der Religionsgeschichte," which outlines his theory on the "convergence of types").

THE PLACE OF STATISTICS

Though there can be hardly any doubt that a full yet cautious use of statistics can be of great use to the sociologist of religion, there has been, at least until recently, a difference in practice between continental and American students. The former have been and are more reluctant to make extensive use of the statistical method: the latter have placed during the earliest decades of the twentieth century a not quite justifiable overemphasis on this approach. Whereas some authors of the former groups arrive at a priori-constructions lacking the broad basis of verifiable facts, the latter school seems to be too reluctant to give that interpretation to their findings which alone can make them really meaningful.

DOCTRINE AND CULT

In the science of religion as it began to take shape since the middle of the nineteenth century a controversy developed regarding the significance and the primacy of different types of expressions of religious experience. The problem of chronological and axiological *priority* of theory (myths, beliefs, ideas, concepts, doctrines, dogmata) and practice (worship, rites, ritual) in religion was discussed by students of different religions and civilizations (W. Robertson Smith, Andrew Lang, Wilhelm Schmidt, Otto Gruppe). The sociologist of religion is vitally interested in striking the right balance and placing adequate emphasis on the various types of expression. As against intellectualism he will insist on the central nature and function of *worship* in its various aspects, named by some the very core of religion; to any neglect and underestimation of the *rational* expression of religious experience he will have to protest by demonstrating its significance as vehicle of the self-interpretation of the religious community. He does not see any necessity to argue for chronological priority of either of the two aspects, bearing in mind their interrelation and mutual stimulation

III

INTER-RELATION OF RELIGION AND SOCIETY

Sociological studies in religion will have to include the whole width and breadth of mankind's religious experience. For practical purposes, the individual sociologist, who has special intents in mind, may have to concentrate on a problem or problems of a given period of the history of civilization and religion, in a specific area or group. In principle, however, no type of devotion or phenomenon of religious significance should be excluded. If the system of the sociology of religion is not broad enough to include them all, something must be wrong with it.

The student of religion must acquaint himself with the research of the *sociologist*. The latter examines the foundation of society—that is, the total and specific environment of the social being in both its positive and negative effect—and psychologically and sociologically meaningful attitudes, as manifested in communality. He analyzes all forms of societal organization and association (typology of communities). He studies the constructive and destructive social forces which determine the dynamics of social life and the patterns of social change, transformation, and revolution in relation to the physical, mental, cultural, and technical environment. Research in abstracto and in concreto supplement each other: general categories are verified in historical and empirical documentation, and individual phenomena are interpreted in the light of such categories.

The student of *religion* can be expected to supply the sociologist with a working theory of religious life and its manifestations. He is concerned with the theologico-philosophical, epistemological, psychological, phenomenological and historical analysis of the nature and meaning of religion and with the forms of expression of religious experience and the dynamics of religious life. Systematic inquiry into the forms and contents of belief, worship, and rites will be based on the study of the religious act and its motivation and meaning. It will be focused on the problem of religious communion and will do justice to the wide variety of types of communal religious life and activity.

The historical and systematical analysis of the inter-relation between religion and general as well as specific environmental factors and conditions (physical, cultural, social) can be successfully undertaken only by close cooperation of the student of religion with the student of society. The former will have to avail himself of the categories worked out in sociological research; the latter will have to give careful attention to the meaning of religious language and terminology. A threefold meaning will have to be recognized: first, the actual meaning of any work and concept, sometimes obscured by tradition and age; secondly, the religious implications of terms like sin, repentance, grace, redemption, etc.: thirdly, the concrete, individual "theological" interpretation given to the term in a religious community (by individual religious leaders). On this basis religious acts like adoration, prayer, and the conduct and attitudes of a cult group will have to be interpreted. There is no hope of grasping the spirit and of understanding the life, symbolism, and behavior of a religious group so long as no serious attempt is made to correlate the isolated traits (concepts, rites, customs) observed with a notion of the central experience which produces them.

As indicated above, *systematic and historical approaches* are both necessary for the study of the religious group, the former aiming at the construction of types of sacred communion, the latter attempting to embrace all the variegated forms religious fellowships have shown under different ethnic, historical, cultural, and social conditions. Worship in the *home* may serve as a simple example. Irrespective of profound differences in general and special environment, cultural level and religious level, the rites conducted in the "homes" of the American Indian, the Egyptian, the Chinese, or the German or Englishman of the sixteenth century have certain features in common, as compared with public, congregational ceremonies. Further proof of the fruitfulness of combined systematic and historical inquiries can be found in the discovery of many similarities in the religious implications of the beliefs and ceremonials at all times surrounding the *sacred* rules in vastly different societies, as well as in a parallel disinclination to corporate rites with *mystics* in practically all great civilizations.

We shall now list the main tasks of a sociology of religion:

THE STUDY OF THE INTERRELATION OF RELIGION AND SOCIETY

What are the main points of contact? Analysis of the nature and structure of society as well as of religion is carried out in the disciplines dedicated to this purpose (general sociology, theology, and philosophy of religion). Inasmuch as it is an interaction which is examined, justice must be done to the influence both of society on religion, and of religion on society.

(a) "Religion" means both experience and its expression in thought and action—in concepts, forms of worship, and organization. It is essential to correlate the expression with the experience to which it testifies. The influence of social forces, structures, and movements on the expression of religious experience is more easily ascertained than their effect upon the experience itself. While some conceive of it in terms of determinism, others are inclined to emphasize the autonomy and independent dynamics of religious life.

A wide field is open for the sociologist of religion in the examination of the sociological roots and functions of myths, doctrines and dogmas, of cultus and association in general and in particular *(hic et nunc)*. To what extent are the different types of the expression of religious experience in different societies and cultures socially conditioned (technological, moral, cultural level)? What is the contribution of social forces to the differentiation of religious life and its forms? To what extent does the latter reflect social stratification, mobility, and differentiation (division of society according to sex, age, occupation, property, rank and prestige)? What of the social background and origins of religious movements and of the leaders and their congregations? What does religion contribute to the

integration and disintegration of social groups? How do eco-
logical factors influence the religious community?

Through the ages different ethnic groups have developed
in the different geographical areas of the world. Societies have
been formed in these areas by these groups. Their activities
resulted in the formation of cultures. With the development
of culture, differentiation within the different societies increased; hence the sociologist of religion has to take into
account the temporal, regional, ethnic, cultural and social
factors. The research of the archaeologist, historian and philologist supplies him with material for the study of religious
groupings from the beginnings of history to the present day.
He is aware of the difference of the anthropogeographical
milieu (climate) in which these groups evolved. He learns from
physical and cultural anthropology about the variety of physical, mental and spiritual endowment and development of the
different ethnic groups. Again the historian, the sociologist,
and political scientist lend him material for the examination
of historical societies and civilizations from the point of view
of his interest.

The five continents are broken down into smaller regional,
cultural and social areas, down to village, house, and family
units. The periods of world history are divided into epochs,
each of which is accentuated by the growth and decline of
historical cultures and societies; in each of these shortlived
tribal units have succeeded each other in the domination of
a given region or section of the populated earth, either simply
co-existing or vying with each other for temporary or semi-
permanent superiority.

What has been the role of religion in these narrowly defined
units? Again it is not the historical question of sequence and
development, of motive and effect which the sociologist of
religion is called upon to answer. He is interested in cross-
sections and in the analysis of structures, in extracting the
typical from the empirical details.

He will not omit considering any primitive society, the
study of which may contribute to his knowledge of the sociology of primitive religion in whatever period or area or

ethnic context it may be found. He will include all that is known of ancient and medieval and modern Oriental cultures and societies (Near, Middle and Far East) and extend his examination of Western society and cultures back beyond the classical world finally to include the successive types developed in the various great periods of the Christian era down to this day. Registering the rise and growth of religious groups, he will proceed to analyze their nature, structure, and constitution and will thus contribute to the typological understanding of religiously motivated grouping. He will compare instances where religious concepts, forces, and personalities effected subtle or far-reaching changes and transformations in the cultural and social context in which they occurred. He will study the activities of religious leaders and groups, forms of action and response, and with the help of the psychologist will ascertain their meaning and motivation. He will be arrested by the similarity, though not the identity, of patterns of behavior, thought, and reaction under often widely different conditions and circumstances, and he will untiringly contribute to a more comprehensive and profound knowledge of the typology of religious thought and feeling, religious ideas, institutions, religious theory and practice.

(b) The *sociologist* is interested in the sociologically significant function and effect of *religion* upon *society*. Granted that religious forms and institutions, like other fields of human and cultural activity, are conditioned by the nature, atmosphere, and dynamics of a given society, to what extent does religion contribute to the cohesion of a social group and to the dynamics of its development and history? It should be borne in mind that because religion conceived of as a vital force transcends its expression, it cannot be unreservedly regarded as one among many spheres of cultural activity. Some are inclined to look upon it as the fountainhead or the matrix of all cultural and social activity of a group of human beings. The theory of the identity of religion with the sum total of man's cultural and social life does not do justice to its peculiar nature. Careful analysis of causes of cultural and social changes reveal the part religion plays in the fomentation of the revolutionary and evolutionary development of society. Of all varieties of social life and grouping within a given society, religious associations of a peculiar and not of the traditional type will arrest the attention of the student. The growth and decline of *specifically* religious organizations and groups is a theme of the greatest importance to the sociologist as well as to the historian of religion. He will investigate the nature and typology of these groups, their structure, and their constitution. Size, character, purpose, relation to the other groups, leadership of the specifically religious group will have to be investigated. What is the function of the different expressions of religious experience in integrating it? Why do these groups present a variety of different forms of organization, and how is the latter related to the self-interpretation of the group?

THE RELIGIOUS GROUP

The religious group is characterized by the nature and order of the basic relationships of its members: in the first place, that of each member to the *numen*; in the second place that of the members to each other. The sociologist of religion will have to examine the character of this twofold relationship in the case of each individual group because the nature, intensity, duration, and organization of a religious group depends upon the way in which its members experience God, conceive of, and communicate with Him, and upon the way they experience fellowship, conceive of, and practice it. Inasmuch as religious communion conversely strengthens religious faith and action, we find a circle—however, not of a vicious nature. The sociologist of religion, interested in the study of a cultic group, cannot be satisfied with reviewing its theology as the foundation of the theory and practice of fellowship among its members. He must probe further, studying the religious experience on which theology and other modes of expression (behavior, rites, language) are based. More than other types of association, a religious group presents itself as a *microcosm* with its own law, outlook on life, attitude and atmosphere. Wherever political, artistic, scientific, or other groups exhibit comparable cohesion and comprehensiveness, they usually can be shown to be of a semi-religious nature. Altogether too frequently students of religious communities have been satisfied to juxtapose findings as to beliefs, customs, and patterns of organization regarded as representative, without correlating them to the central attitudes and the norms characteristic of the group. Yet it is essential to realize that religious communities are constituted by loyalty to an ideal or set of values which is the basis of their communion. In other words, a religious group should not be regarded as just a fellowship of persons drawn together by mutual sympathy of common interest, or even by common ideas and customs. While these factors enter in, they are not basic.

Certain religious communities have been described as units in which parallelism of spontaneity rules. They are not really *typical,* but rather exhibit a minimum of what it takes to form a religious community.

Next to loyalty to an ideal or values postulated by the central religious experience from which the group springs, the degree of intensity of its religious life is decisive. That, too, is at times overlooked by those who are inclined to evaluate the significance of a religious group exclusively by its size and structure. Intensity is a dynamic quality; it will frequently change, it will rise and fall. It is characteristic of some religious groups to sustain a certain, perhaps high, degree of intensity developed early in their history and maintained at an even level, while others pass through varying phases. The intensity of religious experience may find special expression in some one doctrine or practice, or occasionally in several.

In the earlier stages of the study of religious psychology, French, German and American scholars unfortunately concerned themselves primarily with marginal cases of pathologically developed religious temperament. The sociologist of religion must beware of falling into the same error in overemphasizing random phenomena (eccentric forms of sectarianism, etc.) The historical beginnings of religious and sectarian communities, however, are important fields for investigation of the mediums through which religious experience finds expression. The size of a religious group deserves the attention not only of the statistician, but also of all those who believe that a very different psychology typifies the masses on the one hand and intimate circles on the other. The size of the group, however, may be determined entirely by chance and circumstance.

With the group there is a distinction between those members who will engage in religious activity from personal choice or in deference to tradition such as converts and parishoners of a local congregation, and those who are actively religious— temporarily or consistently—such as lay-deacons or the participants in a procession. Interest can be both passive and active, the latter being exceedingly diversified in form, purpose, means, and duration.

The *ideals* and *values* uniting the group may be considered in the first place as the formulation of desires and aspirations, derived from a basic religious experience. As such they have expressive significance. Secondly, they serve as symbols or standards for the religious community. Thirdly, they render expansion, missionary propaganda, and conversion possible by their communicative value. Finally, they serve to integrate the religious community which binds itself to them. They may be either spontaneously formulated, or acknowledged as tradition (successions of waves of conversions and of generations of followers).

More concretely, all religious groups are united by certain convictions—the acknowledgment of the ideals and values just mentioned—formulated loosely or concisely in statements of faith or doctrinal *creeds,* by certain *cultic* acts which tend to develop and strengthen their communion with the deity (rites, sacraments), and by a cultivation of a *fellowship* in the spirit of the ideals professed. The larger the group, the more the need for a renewed and possibly more intimate grouping may be felt. The sociology of the religious group of the second power, to use de Grasserie's terminology (collegia, associations, brotherhoods, oratories and the like), offers a wide open field and should be developed much more than it has been hitherto. Inasmuch as the growth of religious fervor in élite religious groups may lead to hierarchical development (order, sect), the sociologist of religion may combine his study of intensity and size with that of the structure of the group. For this task the criteria elaborated in general sociology will prove helpful. Yet a warning should be voiced against too unguarded an application of terms and viewpoints derived from the sociological study of other human activities.

Two examples will illustrate this point. Observing the practice of a cultic group, the outsider may be inclined to compare the "control" exercised by a religious leader to that in political or economic organizations without realizing that obedience may in each case be very differently motivated, and that it hence may not be really the same thing. Again the term "behavior" is often enough made to cover a variety of forms of conduct, without regard for the intention distinguishing them. Both paying taxes and sharing out of religious motives with one's brother are ways of handing out money, but how differently the acts are motivated and how different the "value"!

The greatest differences and varieties can be found in the *structures* of religious groups.

Though we possess many excellent monographs on the historical development of an infinite number of cults, there is room for much more extensive and intensive study of the typology of the constitutions of religious communities. Corresponding to the twofold level of religious organization, the natural and the specifically religious bases, the order of cultic communities varies. In the first instance and frequently in the second, it is patterned after "secular" models (the father as leader of a cult-group, tribal organization paralleled by cultic set-up). But it may also develop its own forms (monasticism, egalitarianism). The study of the structures of religious groups should be carried on without prejudice in favor of one or the other principle of organization, e.g., the charismatic as against the hierarchical, or vice versa—and application of the general methodological requirement discussed above. Historical orientation should be supplemented by typological investigation.

Constitution may refer to a loose, temporary, undifferentiated set-up, or—with many intermediate stages—to a highly stratified and comprehensive order. The structure of the religious as of most other groups is determined by the division of functions. Such a division is practically ubiquitous from the simplest to the most complex cultic associations. It may consist in an individual occasionally or permanently taking over functions, duties, and responsibilities, with or without corresponding rights, honors, and privileges (prestige).

The degree of differentiation of functions does not necessarily depend upon the general cultural level. Elaborate specialization is found in less advanced societies (West African, Polynesian) and in higher cultures (even in non-conformist Protestant and certain sectarian groups). The process of differentiation of functions within the group may involve specifically religious activities exclusively or may have a broader scope. It may be initiated, recognized, and justified on a pragmatic basis ("useful," "necessary") or on grounds of principle (metaphysical basis, theological explanation). A wide and little cultivated field is open to the investigator in the comparative study of the differentiation of functions, especially in the narrow sense (function in the cultus). Another is the study of the social background and situation of the members composing the group, these factors having a bearing on its nature and structure particularly in the case of transitory phenomena (meeting, festival). The social origin of the group and the composition of its constituency pose two different problems.

Still another is the analysis of the "atmosphere" and the spirit prevailing. There is a sociological basis for the Christian teachings on the "Holy Spirit" and its communication.[32] The atmosphere can be determined by a careful investigation of the central values acknowledged, the attitudes prescribed and practiced in the community, and the development through which it has gone.

What constitutes a church, a denomination, a sect, a society, a confraternity? What is the significance of gradation, authority, order in a religious community? The sociologist of religion will have to answer that question on the basis of broad theological and juridical, historical, psychological, and sociological information. What is the (theological) self-interpretation of the nature and significance of its fellowship, is the first question. The second concerns the historical origin and development, the third, the prevailing spirit (intensiveness, exclusiveness, broadness, compromise) and the general attitude toward the world (identification, withdrawal, critical acceptance, consecration). The student will take into account the immanent development within the cult-community and the impact of outside influences and outside patterns and examples. He will examine the role of intimacy to the first, second, and third power (examples: the circle of Jesus' followers, the renewed intimacy on the basis of the experience of the sixteenth century Reformers, the Pietist group of the seventeenth century, etc.) As far as the constitution of religious groups is concerned we find a variety of principles. There is a subjective and an objective viewpoint. That is, in principle, a community may be universal; actually it may be limited to a certain social, racial or local group of people. There are furthermore universal and selective groups. Changes occur in which nationally or racially limited groups—this limitation may be objective or subjective—are transformed into universal communities. Conversely a universal orientation may be qualified by national, social, or other criteria, as in the case of the national religious bodies in Eastern and Western Christianity, in Islam, and in Buddhism. Various degrees of this "qualification" can be observed (relative isolation, language, youth-problem). The sociologist will be interested in exploring the relationship prevailing between the different subgroups.

Differentiation within the religious group can be conditioned in two ways: by religious and by extra-religious factors. As far as the former is concerned we find a considerable amount of variableness in the nature, intensity, and color of the unifying, basic religious experience, shades or differences in theoretical (belief, myth, doctrine) and practical (worship, activities) expression. They make for differentiation within the practice, tradition, and organization of a religious community in certain periods, locally and otherwise, particularly if combined with the second factor. Extra-religious influences making for differentiation are represented by technical, cultural, social, economic developments, resulting in social stratification according to differences of sex and age, property, occupation and status. Sociologists have here a very important and rewarding task in exploring the effects of these differences upon the religious group. The transformation of devotional attitudes, of concepts, rites and institutions, the rise of new and the decline of old ideas and practices under the impact of these factors with respect to the different religious bodies has not been sufficiently investigated.

The problem of authority, with all its implications, has to be discussed. More comparative study of the foundation upon which authority is supposed to rest, the forms which it may take, the methods by which it works, its execution and its delegation, are necessary. Typologies of religious charisma (founder, prophet, priest, etc.) as outlined by Max Weber, A. Causse, G. van der Leeuw and J. Wach, should be worked out in much the greater detail. The theory of personal and official charisma will prove very fruitful; it has recently, been applied to the study of primitive society, Indo-European and Hebrew religion, and medieval Christianity.

GENERAL AND SPECIFIC SOCIOLOGY OF RELIGIOUS GROUPS

In contrasting origin and development, nature and purpose, structure and attitudes of the religiously motivated group with that of other types of grouping, the sociologist will attempt to define its general characteristics. Although there is room for doubt if such procedure would do justice to the individuality of the historical phenomenon, that is, of the group *hic et nunc*, it must be pointed out that parallelisms and similarities exist which call for investigation. The following examples will illustrate what we mean by such similarities: (1) the general motivation of sharing certain common religious experiences, the differences in content in the latter notwithstanding; (2) the nature of the acts whereby they are expressed; (3) the process of crystallization of religious fellowships around charismatic leadership; (4) the general pattern of the development from simple into complex structures; (5) comparable types of religious authority and of attitudes in religious audiences; (6) parallelism in the reaction of types of cult groups to their environment; (7) differentiation of functions within the group according to general criteria (age, sex, property, occupation, rank).

These parallelisms and resemblances might pertain to a limited number of groups, to be defined by these very similarities (from two to any number), or they may extend from a large number to practically all groups of special type, or to religious groups in general. *Types* may be defined geographically, chronologically, ethically, culturally, or religiously. Thus, the motive of the urge to spread the faith may identify one religious group with many others, while its absence (limitation or rejection of propaganda) distinguishes it from another. Some cult-communities owe their existence primarily to missionary societies, orders, etc., in different religions. Some are of a militant character manifested in the means employed and in their "ideology" in general; others are quieter, more contemplative in nature. In both cases the religious motive is decisive. A great number of Hindu religious groups have some general convictions in common, notwithstanding divergences in theology and cultus; some share forms of devotion, which, however, may be addressed to different deities, and so forth. Christian sects exhibit attitudes which, if contrasted to those of other religious organizations, offer striking parallels. Some use rites not known to others within the same brotherhood of faith, such as the washing of feet, unction, the kiss of peace.

A satisfactory and distinctive *nomenclature* will have to be worked out by the student of the general sociology of religious groups. Terms and categories should preferably be familiar, rather than fanciful new creations ("hierology," "hierosophy," etc.). Yet mistakes must be avoided which may arise from the application of a technical term developed in a distinctive historical, social, cultural, or religious context to a wider range of phenomena.

It is the task of *general sociology* to investigate the sociological significance of the various forms of intellectual and practical expression of religious experience (myth, doctrine; prayer, sacrifice, rites; organization, constitution, authority); it falls to the *specific sociological study* to cover sociologically concrete, historical examples: a Sioux (Omaha) Indian myth, an Egyptian doctrine of the Middle Kingdom, Murngin or Mohammedan prayer, the Yoruba practice of sacrifice, the constitution of the earliest Buddhist Samgha, Samoyed priesthood, etc. Such studies should be carried out for the smallest conceivable units (one family or clan, a local group at a given period of time, the occasional following of one cult leader, etc.). There is no danger of this task turning into a historical, psychological, anthropological, theological undertaking, because the sociological viewpoint will be the decisive one. Thus the philologist would ascertain the meaning of a passage of the Indian Atharva-Veda; the historian would assign it to a period in the cultural, political, and religious development of the Hindu; the psychologist would concentrate on its origin and significance as an expression of feeling and thought; and the anthropologist would deal with it from a folkloristic point of view. The sociologist is interested in its origin and formation, in the structure and meaning of the Hindu community of faith. There can be some doubt as to how the work of the special sociologist of religion should be organized, that is, in which order he would proceed best. Inasmuch as research is carried on in a number of related disciplines, there is no hope that what is most needed always will be taken up first. However, the angles which ought to be of paramount concern to those interested in the systematic development of our field are the temporal, the spatial, the ethnic and cultural, and the religious viewpoint.

(a) The sociologist is interested in religious groups of the past and the present. Though contemporary conditions may claim his attention from the pragmatic point of view, the investigation of phenomena of even the remote past ought not to be neglected (sociology of ancient cults, everywhere). In this emphasis normative philosophy or theology of society on the one hand, and descriptive sociology on the other, differ.

(b) Notwithstanding his interest in the socio-religious situation of the society of which he is a member, the student of religious groups cannot afford to exclude from his range of effort a concern with religious grouping in all parts of the populated earth. Because everything that exists is worth knowing—though not to the same extent—no religious group established anywhere should be omitted in these studies.

(c) The same is equally true of ethnic divisions, cultures and societies. Within a chronological and spatial framework, each tribe and people, each culture and society will find its place. Naturally not all can claim the interest of the student to the same extent as those which stand in a closer or looser relation to the culture or society under investigation. But as long as socio-religious conditions in a major cultural context remain unexplored, the work is not done.

(d) It is understandable that in a Christian society Christian groups will appear the major, though certainly not the exclusive subject of interest to the sociologist of religion. As he is obliged to include all forms of Christian communities, so he will have to extend his studies over the whole field of non-Christian religious grouping in all its varieties. It may be advisable to proceed, if the special viewpoint warrants it, from the nuclear topic interest to wider and wider contexts; to include the study of religious groups, historically or phenomenologically related to Christianity (Greek, Roman, Hebrew), to those typologically similar (Mystery religions, Buddhism), and finally to those of a radically different character. As far as Christian groups are concerned, a great deal remains to be done to bring the investigation of the "lesser" groups up to date. Attention has for a long time been concentrated on all forms of "official" religion, while religiously and sociologically important and interesting groupings within or without have been neglected. Of the non-Conformist groups only the "spectacular" ones have attracted attention. The study of creeds and rites must be supplemented by a thorough examination or organization and constitution, in theory and practice. In this context we have to repeat that the exploration of historical origin and development is no substitute for systematic and typological study.

Selected Bibliography

JAMES, E. O., *The Social Function of Religion* (Nashville: Cokesbury Press, 1940).

LINTON, RALPH, *The Study of Man* (New York: D. Appleton-Century Co., 1936).

NIEBUHR, H. RICHARD, *The Social Sources of Denominationalism* (New York: Henry Holt and Co., 1929).

PINARD DE LA BOULLAYE, HENRI, S. J., *L'étude comparée des religions* (Paris: Gabriel Beauchesne, 1922, 1929, 2 vols.).

SOROKIN, PITIRIM A., *Social and Cultural Dynamics* (New York: American Book Co., 1937–1941, 4 vols.).

TROELTSCH, ERNST, *The Social Teaching of the Christian Churches* (New York: The Macmillan Co., 1931).

VAN DER LEEUW, GERARDUS, *Religion in Essence and Manifestation* (London: G. Allen and Unwin, 1938), Sec. II, B.

WACH, JOACHIM, *Sociology of Religion* (Chicago: University of Chicago Press, 1944).

WALLIS, WILSON D., *Religion in Primitive Society* (New York: F. S. Crofts and Co., 1939).

WEBER, MAX, *Gesammelte Aufsätze zur Religionssoziologie* (Tübingen: J. C. B. Mohr, 1920–1921, 3 vols.).

WEBER, MAX, *Wirtschaft und Gesellschaft* (Tübingen: J. C. B. Mohr, 1921), Sec. III, Chap. IV, "Religionssoziologie."

WIESE, LEOPOLD VON, and HOWARD BECKER, *Systematic Sociology* (New York: John Wiley and Sons; London: Chapman and Hall, 1932).

WILL, ROBERT, *Le culte* (Paris: Félix Alcan, 1925–1929).

RADHAKRISHNAN AND THE COMPARATIVE STUDY OF RELIGION

THE COMPARATIVE STUDY of religions has never been merely an academic concern for the great Hindu scholar to whose philosophy this volume is dedicated. He has been existentially interested in such studies since the days of his youth. In "My Search for Truth," the moving autobiographical sketch which he contributed to a volume entitled *Religion in Transition* (1937), he reports how the challenge by Christian critics of Hinduism, his own faith, impelled him at the time of his student-days at Madras to "make a study of Hinduism and find out what is living and what is dead in it."[1] Again and again in writings, he has traced historically phases of development in Western (Greek and Christian) and Indian (Brahmanic, Hindu and Buddhist) religious thought, and has analyzed in systematic fashion basic notions in Hinduism and Christianity.[2] Moreover, he has devoted at least one part of one of his books[3] to "Comparative Religion." Here he recapitulates briefly the growth of this science, discusses some of the current

115

objections, shows its value, characterizes the spirit in which such study must be undertaken, and finally points up some problems which it must face. Here are some of the convictions to which the comparative study of religions has led the distinguished Hindu thinker: "It increases our confidence in the universality of God and our respect for the human race. It induces in us not an attitude of mere tolerance which implies conscious superiority, not patronizing pity, nor condescending charity, but genuine respect and appreciation."[4]

"The different religions have now come together, and if they are not to continue in a state of conflict or competition, they must develop a spirit of comprehension which will break down prejudice and misunderstanding and bind them together as varied expressions of a single truth."[5] Finally, by investigating parallels and analogies, such study "broadens our vision."[6] In addition to psychological and historical inquiries it poses the philosophical problem of value and validity. "How far can the facts gathered by Comparative Religion be accepted as expressing the reality of an unseen ground?"[7]

This sketch of the nature and the task of a comparative study of religions proves that Professor Radhakrishnan (a) is familiar with the expressions of the age-old quest for a definition of the relation of the different great religions of the world with each other and with the development of the sciences (history) of religion, such as was conceived in the 19th century by Max Mueller and his successors; (b) that he has contributed to our increase of knowledge of several of the great world faiths and their relations with each other; (c) that his studies have convinced him that all religions have developed in a peculiar ethnic, sociological, cultural, and intellectual environment; (d) that he is aware of resemblances and differences in their expressions; (e) that he regards them as "tentative adjustments, more or less satisfactory, to the same spiritual reality, after which the human spirit feels and by which, in some manner, it is acted upon;"[8] (f) that none of them ought to be regarded as "absolute," a conviction which Professor Radhakrishnan shares with E. Troeltsch;[9] (g) that understanding any form of religion requires sympathy and empathy.

The work of the Indian philosopher shows a preoccupation with two of the world religions: Brahmanism and Christianity. Buddhism comes next in his attention and appreciation. There are fewer references to Islam; which is surprising in view of the importance of this religion for the history of India.[10] He rarely refers to what is known as the tribal national religion and the "primitive" cults. The reasons for this preference are partly to be sought in his own personal development (Hindu home, Christian instruction), partly in his primary interest in the intellectual expression of religious experience or, in other words, the philosophical bent of his nature, and, last but not least, in his often voiced conviction that we have to "get behind and beneath all outward churches and religions, and worship the nameless who is above every name."[11] Though he finds this attitude in all parts of the world, especially in the mystics, we are led to believe that Brahmanism, in addition to being the thinker's physical and intellectual home, represents to him very possibly the highest forms of the eternal religious quest of man.

The student of the history of religions will have to ask: Does he do full or adequate justice to both, Brahmanism and Christianity? This question cannot be answered here, inasmuch as it would have to be discussed at length and with considerable documentation. There can be no doubt of the profound insight into the nature and history of Brahmanism and the intimate acquaintance with the religious, literary and political mani-festations of the spirit of India to which Radhakrishnan's *oeuvre* testifies. It is significant, however, that it is the earlier, the Brāhmaṇic phase of Hindu religion, that it is the classical Vedānta, on which he concentrates his attention and which commands his affection and loyalty. It is Śaṅkara's rather than Rāmānuja's version of the Vedānta to which he adheres and it is the Brāhmaṇic phase rather than the medieval form of Hinduism which represents for him "the" religion of India. It is actually a double option which determines Professor Radhakrishnan's explicit and implicit evaluation of religion: his preference for the apprehension of ultimate reality as proclaimed by the seers and sages of India and, within this tradition, his preference for the teachings of the Upaniṣads in the peculiar interpretation of the Advaita school. The philosopher, Western or Eastern, may well agree with this second emphasis; but the scholar interested in the comparative study of religions may well ask if certain other manifestations of Hinduism should not be more fully included when we attempt to discuss the essence of the religion of India. Especially Occidentals seem all too prone to identify the latter with the metaphysics of the Vedānta without doing justice to the characteristic spirit of devotion to which the earlier and later mediaeval documents of Hinduism testify. The work of such scholars as Pope, Grierson, R. Otto, Schomerus and others is not widely enough known. The result is the one-sidedness in the presentation and appraisal of the religion of India which we find in so many publications of Western scholars and amateurs. Few of them betray any familiarity with the work of Bhandarkar, the great pathfinder in the exploration of Viṣṇuism, Śivaism and the minor cults, or of his modern successors.

Let us return once more to the autobiographical sketch in which Radhakrishnan outlines the growth of his interest in the two great religious traditions with which he has been confronted all his life, the Indian and the Christian. It is regrettable that until recently this meant the Indian and the Western. If we recall the identification of Christianity and the West in the minds of Occidentals and—hence—in the minds of the peoples of the East throughout the Victorian age and into the 20th century, 'we shall better understand the critical attitude towards Christianity which Professor Radhakrishnan's writings betray. Or rather, we shall appreciate even more highly the untiring efforts on the part of this great Hindu scholar to do justice to Christianity. From the days of his youth he had met with a form of Christian apologetic which could be nothing if not ineffective and which could only have adverse effects upon him, because it was uninformed and proceeded from unexamined presuppositions. Not that the conviction on the part of Christians that Christ, rightly understood, is "the light of the world" would have had to be offensive; but the claim that Hinduism, whatever its form, was all darkness and that Christianity, whatever its expression, is all light. The advocates of this latter doctrine all too frequently were prone to forget how woefully deficient, how necessarily limited by their own background, their understanding and interpretation of the *kerygma* of Christ was, how compromised by colonialism, provincialism, and conventionalism. Not that the truly Christian spirit and the splendid achievements of many selfless workers for the cause of Christ in India and elsewhere could be denied by anyone; but many Westerners conceived of the meeting between Christian and Hindu as entirely a one way traffic, which consisted in condescendingly presenting for total acceptance a parcel in which the gospel was wrapped in sheets often not as clean as could be desired. All this one has to bear in mind if the reaction which many highly educated Indians have been exhibiting to efforts of this kind is to be understood and properly assessed. There is a notable trace of bitterness in a great number of references to Christianity in Radhakrishnan's writings. Here he speaks as the apologist of Hinduism, that is, of Hinduism as he interprets it, of a reconstructed Hinduism, or better, of the ideal of Hinduism.

I am not sure that he always applies the same procedure—carefully distinguishing between the empirical and the ideal—when he discusses what is to him the great religion of the West. Granted that there are valid reasons for the criticism which he voices in the section on Christian Missions and Indian faiths. However, I find little evidence that he considers the Christian faith seriously as a live option for India. To reject unwarranted attempts as "Westernization" or, for that matter, any imposition of "foreign" notions is one thing; however, the only alternative to such attempts is not necessarily the somewhat relativistic idea of *sharing*. "The different religious men of the East and the West are to share their visions and insights, hopes and fears, plans and purposes." True, this is desirable; but in which spirit, and why not in the Spirit of Christ? The West does not possess a monopoly on Him. Before Him there is neither Jew, nor Greek, nor Indian. The God

of justice and love of whom he testified is either truly our—
and that is for *all* of us "our"—creator and redeemer or not
the true God at all. There is a profounder difference than
Radhakrishnan seems to be willing to admit between tribally
or nationally bound Brāhmaṇic Hinduism and the constitu-
tionally universal message of Christ. But this is not the difference of the faith of one part of the world as over against
that of another.[12] There is no reason why Indian Christians
should not teach any number of Western Christians a deeper
insight into the *kergyma* of the Christ who judges all.

Or is Radhakrishnan merely objecting to the *methods* by
which Christianity so often has sought converts? It could seem
so; because he does not level as harsh a criticism against
Buddhism, another universal faith, as he does against Christianity. After all, to find the truth in Christ and in his teachings
need not prevent anyone from studying with profit and admiring the thought of the great Indian sages. In fact, whoever
expects important contributions from Indian Christianity to
Christian theology and philosophy will have every reason to
familiarize himself with those sages' search for truth.

However, it is not necessarily in the realm of intellectual
endeavor—monumental though Hindu contributions in this
field may be—certainly not *merely* in this realm, that one
would seek and find unexpected treasures. Religion is above
all *devotion*, and the intensity and fervor of the devotional life
of India's saints must put many lukewarm Western Christians
to shame. Here we feel that much that is admirable can be
found in Medieval Hinduism alongside of other things which
are gross and perhaps even repellent.

The sincere and relentless effort to understand the religion
of peoples different from our own is certainly highly desirable.
Radhakrishnan himself is an eminent example of such endeavor. Yet we do not feel that it is all said with the simple
formula: let us share. The problem of *validity* and of *truth* has
to be faced, as the author of *East and West in Religion* himself
reminds us. We agree with him: "revelation is a universal gift,
not a parochial possession."[13] But we cannot follow him when
he continues: "with regard to religions, the question is not of

truth or falsehood but life or death.''[14] It is right to say that
"every living religion has its part in the spiritual education of
the race,''[15] but these parts are not necessarily equal. We feel
that William Temple, who was a believer in universal revelation, made an admirable distinction in saying, "all therefore
is alike revelation; but not all is equally revelatory of the divine
character.''[16] In great fairness Radhakrishnan distinguishes
between the early forms and later developments of both,
Christianity and the religions of India. He contrasts the "pure
and simple teachings of Jesus" with the developments which
Christianity has undergone in the West.[17] In his analysis of
the role of intellectualism, scholasticism, social solidarity, and
activism, and of their historic causes, there is much truth. Yet
some of the more recent investigations in the field of New
Testament exegesis and theology do not quite confirm the
picture he draws of the "religion of Jesus." It is doubtful if
we have a right to say that "he founded no organization, but
enjoined only private prayer.''[18] There is no reference here
to the passion and crucifixion, the central events in the life
of Jesus, the supreme tests of his teaching. Of these, which
for the Christian are of paramount importance as the incomparable instances of divine love and suffering, it cannot be
said that they, as "the characteristics of intuitive realization,
nondogmatic toleration, insistence on non-aggressive virtues
and universalist ethics, mark Jesus out as a typical Eastern
seer.''[19] The Christian is convinced that Jesus was something
else and something more than that. For the Christian the
cardinal question remains: *What do you think of Christ?*[20] Hence
this Christian will not be satisfied with the prospect of a time
when "faith in God and love of man will be the only requisites
for mutual fellowship and service." For the Christian who
deserves the name, belief in Christ and in his spirit is not
something which is added to other basic beliefs and which
can, therefore, be omitted; rather, it is the one central affirmation by which alone all others receive their meaning. It
should be said in all fairness that a majority of Christians
themselves do not see this vital point too clearly. In his chapter,
"The Meeting of Religions," in *Eastern Religions and Western*

Thought, Radhakrishnan remarks that "the man of faith, whether he is Hindu or Buddhist, Muslim or Christian, has certainty," but he adds: "yet there is a difference between the pairs."[21] Faith, he says, for the Hindu does not mean dogmatism, implying that for the Christian it does.[22] But a Christian would have no difficulty in subscribing to the statement that "it is not historically true that in the knowledge of truth there is of necessity great intolerance."[23] He would agree with the Indian thinker that "religion is a matter of personal realisation"; although Radhakrishnan seems to consider this as a typically Hindu attitude,[24] and would most certainly hold that "one's religiousness is to be measured not by one's theological affirmations but by the degree to which one brings forth the fruit of the spirit."[25] However, it is difficult to follow the author of *Eastern Religions and Western Thought* in his protest against the "view of Christ as 'the only begotten son of God' " who "could not brook any rival near the throne."[26] Should Christ, too, then, be regarded—by Christians—as merely one "symbol" among others? It does by no means follow that to accept Christ for what he claimed to be must lead to intolerance and to the persecution of others. Certainly, "no doctrine becomes sounder, no truth truer, because it takes the aid of force."[27]

It is in the concluding paragraphs of his chapter on "The Meeting of Religions" that Radhakrishnan invites Christians to cease propagating their faith. He rightly objects to Karl Barth's denial of universal revelation. It is not in defense of Barthian theology, therefore, or because we believe that "only one religion provides divine revelation and others have nothing of it,"[28] or because we regard the Christian religion as unique,[29] that we hold that ours cannot be the way which this Indian scholar suggests. He cites with approval the example of the Syrian Christians in India—as well as the Hindus, who are "opposed to proselytism."[30] However, to surrender all attempts of inviting and winning others to the cause of Christ, would actually be to deny him. This is not to advocate "religious imperialism." Responsible religious leadership—such as the recent meetings of the International Missionary Council, to which Radhakrishnan himself refers,[31] represent—is well aware that there are pressing tasks which require the wholehearted cooperation of the faithful of all religions. Surely,

> if we do not bring together in love those who sincerely believe in God and seek to do his will, if we persist in killing each other theologically, we shall only weaken men's faith in God. If the great religions continue to waste their energies in a fratricidal war instead of looking upon themselves as friendly partners in the supreme task of nourishing the spiritual life of mankind, the swift advance of secular humanism and moral materialism is assured.[32]

There is much more mutual contact, exploration, exchange, and understanding necessary among the sincere followers of all faiths than is now in evidence. We must, indeed, all recognize the insufficiency of our interpretation of the meaning of faith within our own religious community. This has already been pointed out above. But a Christian would not be contributing his best, if he would not make manifest, in word and in deed, upon what spiritual food he feeds, where he has found the springs of hope, of joy, and of strength. Surely, he should expect the Hindu, the Buddhist, and the Moslem to do likewise. In this area grave errors and many sad mistakes of the past will have to be undone. It is when each believer opens himself completely that he witnesses most honestly. There is no more reason why an Easterner should not accept Christ as readily and as naturally as a Westerner. Christ, the Buddha, Muhammad—we are beginning to understand this better today than did the nineteenth century—are *universal options.* It is wrong for a Hindu to say that these names stand for provincialism. The interpretation of their teaching or the failure to act in conformity with that teaching may often be provincial. It is wrong for a Westerner to say: because my forbears were Christians, I had better be one also. No less a theologian than Søren Kierkegaard has pointed out how difficult it is for a Christian, that is to say, for one brought up in and hence "accustomed" to Christianity, to become a Christian. Modern determinism assumes many subtle forms: one is cultural determinism. Many anthropologists, sociologists, and psychologists—even philosophers—regard religion merely as an expression or a function of civilization. That means that I confess a religion because it happens to be the prevailing one in the culture or society to which I happen to belong. Should we not respect a Westerner who, out of conviction, turns Buddhist or Moslem higher than a *soi-disant* "Christian"? And is not, therefore, the mutual understanding and hence communion of Arab, Hindu, Chinese, and Western Christians profounder than that based merely on mutual "toleration"? It would be difficult to prove to a Ceylonese or to an African Christian that he is wrong if he hopes, prays, and works for the acceptance of Christ by all men.

Radhakrishnan has devoted a chapter to Hindu thought and Christian doctrine in his book on *The Heart of Hindusthan* (1932). There he points out that he finds the same fundamentals emphasized in all religions, namely "that God is; that man stands in some relation to God; and that intercourse of some kind is possible between God and man who has in him the desire to be in harmony with God."[33] It is not difficult to agree with this statement, even if one considers it possible to go beyond the three points in the enumeration of "universals" in religion.[34] But for the reasons stated above, objections must be raised to the explanation—or at least to the phrasing of it—Dr. Radhakrishnan gives for the differences among "the living progressive religions of the world." They relate, according to him, to "accents and emphases, which are traceable to social environment and historic circumstances." This formulation sounds highly relativistic and evades altogether the problem of truth. More specifically, however, it has to be said that the Hindu philosopher does not quite do justice to the difference which exists between the Indian concept of Avatars and the Christian notion of the "Son of God." The view that "Jesus is an avatar,"[35] which has recently been elaborated by Radhakrishnan's fellow countryman, Swami Akhilananda, in his book, *The Hindu View of Christ*, implies the denial that "He had a special relation to God, which it is not possible for others to acquire," and cannot, therefore,

be accepted by those who see in Christ the supreme manifestation of the Divine love; which does not exclude other
manifestations but supersedes them. If the life and passion of
Jesus Christ reveals as much of the nature and purpose of
God as Christians believe it does, it is inadmissible to grant
that as much of that nature and purpose is made known in
any of the various "incarnations" of Viṣṇu, Rāma, Kṛṣṇa, *et
al.* Even the most pronouncedly Johannine understanding of
the life and work of Christ and of the destiny of man, for
whom he died, would not permit us to say that "the resources
of God which were available to him are open to us, and if
we struggle and strive even as he did, we will develop the
God in us."[36] Radhakrishnan thinks that it is "a pious delusion"
to think that "none else than Jesus attained this consciousness
of spiritual oneness with God." I wonder why anyone should
call himself a "Christian," if he does not hold this "uniqueness"
to be true. It does not follow that, if the light of God blazed
forth in such unique splendor in Jesus—as Radhakrishnan puts
it very beautifully—we should not object if the followers, "say,
of Confucius and of Buddha, set up similar claims for their
heroes." Actually, the followers of Confucius have never made
such a claim. And as concerns the founder of Buddhism, we
feel that at this point a real *decision* between Christ and the
Buddha is demanded, not just a simple addition. The issues
which make such a decision necessary, implying quite fundamental differences as they do, cannot be discussed here.[37]

Our distinguished Hindu philosopher rightly states that
"God has never said his last word on any subject; he has
always more things to tell than we now can hear (John 16,
12)." But this does not mean that we are not called upon to
respond to God's previous invitation which he extended to
all men when He became incarnate in Christ or that we should
not see everything that came before, has come since, and will
come, in the light of this His, until now—we cannot say more,
but also certainly not anything less—supreme revelation. This
view, it might be reaffirmed again, does not exclude the
recognition of deep spiritual insight won by and of revelatory
grace granted to Christian and non-Christian seers, prophets,

and saints. Rather, it demands such an interpretation. We whole-heartedly agree with William Temple: "Only if God is revealed in the rising of the sun in the sky, can He be revealed in the rising of a son of man from the dead; only if He is revealed in the history of Syrians and Philistines"—and we add: in the history of the Indians—"can He be revealed in the history of Israel."[38] But that is by no means the same as Radhakrishnan's assertion: "Hinduism believes that every guru is a Saviour, in as much as he quickens in his disciples the life of God and develops the seed of the spirit capable of fructifying in them. Any one who helps us to a complete harmonisation of the finite will of man with the perfect will of God has the power to save us."[39] The present writer has found great inspiration, much truth, wisdom, and beauty, fervent witness to the *numinous* character of ultimate reality in the great Hindu writings through the ages, and hopes to learn still more from them; but he cannot agree with Radhakrishnan's conclusion that "Jesus' own testimony, philosophical truth and religious experience alike demand that He should be brought in line with the other great saints of God, who has not left himself without a witness in any clime or age."[40] True enough; but "neither is there salvation in any other name: for there is none other name under heaven given among men whereby we must be saved." (Acts 4, 12) It may be the case, as this great Hindu thinker intimates, that for some time now a "more critical attitude towards the divinity of Jesus" has been developing among Christian theologians of the West, "who are tending to emphasize more and more his [Jesus'] humanity."[41] However, tendencies in modern Western theology stand in need of evaluation. The mentioned trend has not remained unopposed and, if we are not mistaken, is of late being reversed quite decidedly. Theologians are only a part, and very possibly not the major part, of the Church— and by that we do not mean the ecclesiastical, denominational, and sectarian institutions, but the Great Church of which it was said by its master that the gates of Hell shall not prevail against it. This Christian Church, which started with the confession: Jesus Christ is Lord, will abide by this confession, lest it betray its true foundation. It does not have to subscribe to any of the "classical" theories of the Atonement; but Radhakrishnan's suggestion that it should forget about the notion that "God was in Christ reconciling the world unto himself"[42] it cannot possibly heed. Nor will it be ready to admit that "the sacrifice of Christ has no significance for man as a propitiation for sin."[43]

Some will protest that statements such as these are "dogmatic." However, such characterization would be correct only if these formalizations had no experiential roots. Here they are introduced as the expression of a living experience. "A man's religion," Radhakrishnan rightly observes, "must be his own and not simply accepted on trust or imposed by authority."[44] It is readily granted that otherwise, if they were merely the results of mechanical indoctrination, they would possess little or no validity. What kind of validity *do* they possess except that of being a witness to some subjective experience which might be contradicted and, as some would say, invalidated by expressions of different or even contrary "convictions"? The criterion cannot be the strength or power of the belief. It rather appears to be the degree to which, in and through the experiences to which these statements point, there is effected an actual deepening and widening of spiritual insight into the nature of ultimate reality, of human existence and of the destiny of man. The possibilities which such experiences entail are potentially open to *everyone*. There is nothing esoteric or exclusive about them. Those who believe in a genuine democracy of the spirit will not be afraid of or adverse to contests from which no "competition" will be excluded and where the *true* will prevail.

We come to the crux of the matter when we confront the Hindu scholar's statement with regard to the Indian branch of this Church in which he expects to "*combine* the best elements of Hinduism with the good points of Christianity."[45] An evaluation of the implications of this statement will lead both to an affirmative and a negative conclusion. Neither Hinduism nor Christianity, as we have intimated before, will or ought to remain as it is. We are one with the Indian thinker in stressing the necessity of theological and philosophical "re-thinking" (to use W. E. Hocking's term) in the universal search for truth. But a combination in the sense of mere addition, even in the sense of a synthesis of the Hindu and Christian religions, seems unfeasable. We have elsewhere[46] indicated why, from our point of view, the concept of a "world faith" on a syncretistic basis is not a live option. The crux of the matter, in a very real sense of the word, is indicated by the question: What do you think of Christ? Ever since Jesus' life and work has revealed to man the great two alternative possibilities, it has been impossible to *bypass* this question. But there are no monopolies for West or East, Jew or Greek, for high or low, for rich or poor, as far as the interpretation of the implications of the supreme act of God's redeeming love are concerned. At this point all, wherever found and whoever they may be, are called upon to respond and to contribute their deepest feeling, their profoundest thought, and their most concentrated efforts in action to testify that they are truly redeemed.

We have indicated in an earlier part of this paper that we thoroughly agree with Radhakrishnan in the unqualified rejection of any use of compulsion in spiritual matters. It indicates a lack of confidence in the power of truth, if directly or indirectly force is applied in the service of a religious cause. If we speak of the "great invitation" to accept Christ as one's master, we are not advocating any "*coge intrare*." The only means open to us are an effective example and the winsome word. It is understandable that, in view of vast and grievous mistakes in the past, considerable apprehension exists in the souls and minds of non-Christians—in the West and in the East—lest they be subjected to reprisals, discriminations, and persecutions for not "conforming." Christians must feel a deep sense of shame that many of the peoples of the East have begun to feel secure only after they have won their political independence. But it might also mean that to accept Christ has again become a test or a risk rather than an insurance or a matter of material and social advantage. Moreover, the difference of the situation in the East and in the West is now not much more than one of degree, inasmuch as it takes courage in the Occident too to want really to be a Christian. To guard against any possible misunderstanding I want to reiterate my insistence that our considerations pertain to the realm of the spiritual quest for truth. They are in no way meant to endorse any form of coercion.

The author does not wish to conclude this brief discussion of some points in the writings of Radhakrishnan which seem to him of a controversial nature without adding some remarks of a different character. It may seem picayune to pick out sentences, formulations, or passages in books of a scholar or thinker whose total work is of such imposing character and which testifies to so noble and profound a spirit in its author as that of Sir Sarvepalli Radhakrishnan. The present writer owes much to the beautifully written studies, in philosophy and religion, of the most outstanding living Indian thinker, one whose guiding star throughout has been the quest for truth. By virtue of these commitments he is entitled to expect a similar approach on the part of anyone who becomes his attentive reader. How lengthy would this essay have become, if it would have listed the theses, negative and positive, with which the writer is in profound agreement, such, for example, as the role which Radhakrishnan assigns to religious experience, and his criticism of scepticism, radical materialism, environmentalism, and behaviourism! He is also in full accord with the definition: "Religion is, in essence, experience of or living contact with ultimate reality."[47] This author is aware of the mighty advance which Radhakrishnan's studies in the history of thought represent over the provincial outlook of so many Western and Eastern presentations of the development and the various types of philosophy and religion. He is conscious of the magnificent way in which Radhakrishnan upholds the ideals of justice, of order, and of freedom. There could be no more impressive attempt to combine love for one's country with the desire sympathetically to understand the genuine aspirations and achievements of other nations and civilizations. What remarkable insight and appreciation are revealed in some of his portraits of outstanding leaders in the intellectual and spiritual world of men! No aspect of civilization is overlooked in his studies in Eastern and Western life, past and present.

It would be a rewarding task, though one for which this essay has no place, to attempt to trace and assess the influences which various movements and trends in the Western intellectual world have had upon Radhakrishnan's thinking through the years. Some such influences are detectable in the ideas with which this paper has been concerned: his notion of the nature, the task, and the significance of the comparative study of religions. The frequency with which the distinguished thinker himself refers to this subject seems to indicate that it is one to which he attaches considerable importance. There is, moreover, a great and lively interest in these problems today. That may justify our choice of topic and the insistence upon some considerations with regard to which a weighty question remained in the mind of at least one reader of Radhakrishnan's books.

RELIGION IN AMERICA

The Sociological Approach to Religion
and Its Limits

IN THIS PAPER I propose first to survey a number of approaches to the study of religious groups; then to discuss the nature of religious groups in America and elsewhere; and finally to give a few illustrations of different types of religious groups from the American scene. What I want to do is to suggest an answer to the question: How should we study religious groups and movements?

I

There are several ways to study religion and religions. Since we are interested in investigating the role of religion in Amer-

NOTE: As noted in the introduction, this essay is a composite based on lecture notes. Like other composites—the works of Aristotle are probably the most famous example—it does not read as fluently as Wach's published writings. The essay is very instructive, however, in showing how Wach, as a historian of religions, would approach a topic that is discussed today from a variety of different viewpoints, but not often from the viewpoint of the history of religions.

ica, it may not be out of place to discuss some of them here. First there is the *historical* approach. This approach attempts to trace the origin and growth of religious ideas and institutions through definite periods of historical development and to assess the role of the factors with which religion interacted during these times. Frequently such work presupposes *philological* and even *archeological* research. Without the painstaking work of linguists and archeologists, the early religious history of humankind and many of its later manifestations would have remained unknown or would be inaccessible to us. As a matter of fact, our own religious heritage constitutes first of all a historical problem. Grammatical and historical interpretation will always remain an indispensable element in the study of religion when we try to approach it through the past. But this kind of interpretation does not constitute the only avenue of approach.

It is also legitimate to study the interior aspect(s) of religious experience. Individual and group feelings as well as their dynamics have to be explored. This is the task of *psychological* interpretation. Though in the past decades there has been an appreciable cooling off of the fervor displayed at the beginning of the twentieth century by the advocates of the psychology of religion, still today the various schools of depth-psychology and psychoanalysis offer clues to the understanding of the unconscious and its workings. Allport, Horney, Menninger, and Fromm all have applied Freudian and Jungian theories to the study of religion.

To these methods several new ones have been added. In France and in Germany the so-called *sociology* of religion has evolved. Originally the application of methods of general sociology, such as A. Comte and L. von Stein had outlined, was tied closely to the evolving economic interpretation which Lasalle and Marx had conceived. This approach was corrected by the founders of the modern sociology of religion: Fustel de Coulanges and Emile Durkheim, Max Weber and Ernst Troeltsch, Werner Sombart and Max Scheler. I shall say more about sociology presently. Finally, there emerged in this century still another school, opening up a new avenue to the investigation of religious phenomena: *phenomenology*. Originally conceived as a strictly philosophical discipline with the purpose of limiting and supplementing the purely psychological explanation of the processes of the mind, the phenomenological approach was applied to the study of religion by Max Scheler, Rudolf Otto, and Gerardus van der Leeuw. It aims at interpreting religious ideas, acts, and institutions "as they present themselves," giving due consideration of their "intention" and apart from any preconceived philosophical, theological, metaphysical, or psychological theory. Phenomenology thus provides a necessary supplement to a purely historical, psychological, or sociological approach.

The bridge between the empirical and phenomenological research, on the one side, and the normative, on the other, is supplied by still another approach: *typology*. The endless variety of phenomena that history, psychology, and sociology of religion provide must be organized. Typological studies are designed to do just that. There emerge types of religious leaders—whose lives the historian has illumined, whose intellectual and emotional makeup the psychologist has investigated, and whose social role the sociologist has explored—as well as types of religious groupings and religious institutions. Wilhelm Dilthey, William James, Max Weber, and Howard Becker have masterfully employed this method. Yet, typology is not sufficient in itself. Being of a systematic character, the typological quest is related to both *philosophical* and *theological* inquiries. While a typological analysis refrains from raising the question of truth, the philosopher and especially the theologian will have to deal with and answer that question. (Historical, psychological, sociological, and phenomenological investigations proceed along descriptive lines; philosophy and theology are normative. It will always be an important methodological issue to determine the relationship between descriptive and normative concerns. It goes without saying that the study of religion is vitally interested in this issue.)

Let me illustrate what I have been saying with an example. In the last decade or two we can detect that the American public is becoming increasingly interested in sectarianism. By sectarianism I do not mean denominationalism but the "Small Sects," as Elmer T. Clark has called them. Some of them have been treated by Charles Braden in a volume entitled *These Also Believe.* In this presentation quite a few movements such as Father Divine's Peace Mission, Psychiana, New Thought, I Am, Mormonism, and others are "discussed," that is, their history, their teachings, and their practices are delineated and the reader is left to draw his own conclusions. The question of truth is not raised, normative considerations are strictly excluded. "It will be noted, that there is here stated no purpose to evaluate the movements to show where they are right or wrong, strong or weak" (p. 10). The writer says that "he holds no brief for any particular cult nor is he violently opposed to any" (p. 11). In other words, he would cut the task of the student of religion down to a historical, psychological, and sociological size, shorn of all systematic concern. Now it is true that these methods all are indispensable. They constitute what we call the essence of critical Western scholarship. But it is my thesis that they need to be balanced by attempts to do justice to the meaning of the phenomena under investigation and that it is, therefore, necessary to interpret them in terms of their philosophical and religious relevance.

All this would mean that in order to *understand* a religious movement or institution integrally, we would have to make a careful study of the sources, its origin and its development, of the movement in itself and in interaction with the culture and society, and possibly with the religious community in which it is found. We would study the emotional or affectual make-up of the community and/or its members, which would include the reactions to the outside world. To this we would add a sociological analysis, the aim of which is to explain the social background, to describe the structure, and to ascertain the sociologically relevant implications and results of the movement or institution. This inventory still does not include an examination of the internal consistency of the features that make up the theoretical, the practical, and the sociological expression of the experience of the religious community in question, nor does it include an inquiry into the rational arguments set forth in support of its tenets. The philosopher may legitimately claim competence to judge the consistency and coherence of the propositional elements contained in the doctrines held by the group. Both he and the theologian as "philosophers of religion" are concerned with the epistemological question as to the nature and sources of religious knowledge. But it is the theologian who alone can be expected to respond positively or negatively to religious claims, to raise the question of truth, and to pass judgment on the adequacy and value of religious symbols and concepts, words and deeds.

In this lecture I am concerned with the *sociological* study of religion, its rights and assets, its dangers and its limitations. It was the mistake of those who discovered and pioneered this method to believe that it represented the universal key to understanding religious phenomena. The ideologies of Comte, Marx, and Spencer shared this error. Many of their followers were and are inclined to substitute for the questions of meaning, value, and truth, an inquiry into the social *origin,* the sociological *structure,* and the social *efficacy* of a religious group or movement. American social scientists are very prone to proceed along these lines. Yet, William James has already insisted that the origin of a phenomenon does not have a decisive bearing on its *value*—and what he stipulated for the psychological quest is valid also for the sociological. Even as knowledgeable a study as Richard Niebuhr's *The Social Sources of Denominationalism* labors under the error that the social "milieu" out of which religious movements grow determines their character. Yet, there can be no doubt that it is characteristic of religious experience to transcend cultural conditions, as the same scholar has documented so well in his essays in *Christ and Culture.* It is not possible to derive the characteristic theological teachings of the Church of the Latter-Day Saints or the Shakers from the investigation of the social status of its founders. I find traces of environmentalism even in the assessment of American religion that H. W. Schneider gives in his *Religion in 20th Century America.*

Nevertheless, the sociological approach to the study of religion has great rewards. After a period of unqualified individualism it has reminded us of the importance of *corporate* religion. It has helped to correct the rationalistic prejudice that only the *intellectual* expression of religious experience counts. The rediscovery of the central place of worship in every religion that deserves the name was facilitated by sociological studies. While previously historians had been prone to concentrate their attention on the state as the primary or even the sole factor of importance in historical development, it was the merit of sociological inquirers to have opened up the wide field of social grouping, of covenanting and associating in which religious motivation plays so significant a part. Of course, the influence of religious ideas, practices, and institutions upon society had always intrigued the historians, but it could be assessed better from the time that the organizations of society, to use Dilthey's terminology, were more clearly distinguished from the systems of cultural objectification (law, art, science). But it did take a while before the role of one of these organizations, namely, that of economics in society, was clearly recognized and defined. Liston Pope has written in "Religion and the Class Structure" in *Annals of the American Academy*, vol 91: "Religion, despite the close association of its institutions with the class structure, is neither simply a product nor a cause, a sanction or an enemy, of social stratification. It may be either or both, as it has been in various societies at various times." Here lies the importance of the work of Max Weber and Ernst Troeltsch who corrected the one-sidedness of the approach of Marxist theory. New ground, not really covered by either historians or theologians previously, was broken when sociologists of religion asked about the influence of societal factors upon religion. (Because his contribution in this respect is not often referred to in the literature on the subject, I mention here the important lectures of Jacob Burckhardt, translated under the title *Force and Freedom*, with their discussion of the interaction of religion, culture, and the state.) The study of the influence of social stratification upon religious grouping and on the structure and constitution of religious communities could now supplement the efforts of the church historians and ecclesiastical legalists. This study has been undertaken in Germany, France, and in this country and has yielded many interesting results. Emile Durkheim, Max Weber, Howard Becker, and others have pioneered in this field. But equally important has been the sociological approach to the study of the *religious group,* systematically and typologically organized, thus supplementing historical and psychological investigations. In Christian and non-Christian religions one of the central concerns is communion, *fellowship.* The definition of its nature in the self-interpretation of the religious group is one of the cardinal tenets of faith. Ecclesiology and what corresponds to it in the free bodies is its expression, which the sociologists have to take seriously. Comparison has become possible only since a richer inventory was supplied by many painstaking historical monographs. Compilations such as Ph. Schaff's *Creeds of Christendom,* Neve's *Churches and Sects,* Frank S. Mead's *Handbook of Denominations,* Marcus Bach's *They Found a Faith,* E. T. Clark's "Small Sects, the Study of Organized Religion in the United States," in the *Annals of the Academy of Political and Social Science,* W. W. Sweet's *The American Churches,* and H. W. Schneider's *Religion in 20th Century America* provide lists and summary descriptions of the groups that compose the American religious scene. Instead of being limited to the work of historians of the respective religious communities themselves we are now in the position to define more clearly the nature of the *ecclesiastical body,* the *denomination,* and the *sect.* We begin to understand that not all is said and done when the historical, and that often means accidental, development and the incidents that gave rise to a particular group are taken into consideration. Typical factors of a psychological and sociological nature are of considerable consequence, for example, the typical make-up of the potential sectarian or of the sectarian leader, of the sectarian audience, of the urban parishioner, and of the ecclesiastical bureaucrat. Thus, a categorical scheme becomes visible that may prove helpful in any attempt to do justice to the concrete, individual group under study. But the scheme sociologists of religion use is, as yet, not differentiated, not fine and detailed enough.

Otherwise we would not be so embarrassed by certain phenomena that seem to resist classification and understanding. Are the groups that originated from the so-called Left Wing Reformation solely set apart by their history or do they stand, as Friedman, Littell, and others have attempted to show, for definite theological and ecclesiological doctrines? Is the Church of the Latter-Day Saints a *Christian* ecclesiastical body? What about Father Divine's Peace-Mission? Is the Society of Friends a denomination or a sect? What are the Rosicrucians? In each of these cases, a careful historical study of the origin and growth of the movement is helpful, even indispensable, but no one approach by itself provides the answers. Neither does a psychological inquiry, though it will shed some light. It is an error, or worse, it is arrogance for some psychologists—I shall name here only Erich Fromm—to believe that they actually understand the motivation of a religious group or person without a more thorough training in religious studies than they often possess. An examination of a sociological nature will reveal the type to which the particular group belongs. That is, it will correct a one-sided emphasis on the ideology (theology) or the forms of worship, both of which in the eyes of the historian have often stood out.

A religious group may resemble other types of groups (political, artistic, economic, and intellectual associations) in many ways. That will be true especially of the communities I have called natural groups, that is, those in which natural (blood) and religious ties are identical. It is less true of specifically religious organizations that are held together primarily or exclusively by cultic bonds. Yet, it is highly important to do justice to the nature of the *religious* group as such. Failure to do that has marred many sociological studies since the beginning of the twentieth century.

II

In every group that lays claim to the title "religious," the paramount fact is the religious experience that nourishes and sustains it. We define religious experience as a confrontation by man with Ultimate Reality—for no finite or relative phenomenon is worthy of adoration, only God is.

Religious experience traditionally has expressed itself in three ways: in thought, in action, and in fellowship. However, it would be a great mistake to look upon the expression in fellowship as one that may or may not be added to a full expression in belief and cultus. All three forms are constitutive, and only in fellowship can the two others, the intellectual and the practical, attain their true meaning. Myth or doctrine are the articulation in thought of what has been experienced in the confrontation with Ultimate Reality; and cultus is the living out of this confrontation in action. Both give direction to the community, formed by those who are united in a particular religious experience, and this community is actively shaping and developing its religious experience in thought and in action.

The religious *act* will always be *somebody's* religious act. Modern Western man is all too prone to think of the solitary individual first and last. Yet, the study of primitive religions shows that, by and large, religion is a group affair, individual experiences notwithstanding. One of its keenest students, R. R. Marett, puts it thus: "Primarily and directly, the subject, the owner as it were, of religious experience is the religious society, not the individual" (*Threshold of Religion*, p. 137), and: "The religious society rather than the religious individual must be treated as primarily responsible for the feelings, thoughts and actions that make up historical religion" (ibid., p. 123). In most important ceremonies a large number of people must participate. There is no denying that on a higher level of civilization a more strongly individualized attitude develops: not only the outstanding individual (king, priest) but the average devotee will cultivate his own communion with the numen, say his own special prayers, and perform his personal worship. That is eminently the case in the great world religions. Nevertheless, all through the history of religions the thought and action of one man have been indissolubly tied to the thought and action of another. The old phrase, *Unus Chris-*

tianus nullus Christianus—"one Christian is no Christian," holds true of all other religions, too. Many minds of possibly many generations help to weave a myth, and a doctrine results from the reflection and deliberation of an often long line of religious thinkers. It takes an equally long time before, through the cooperation of generations of members, a ritual has evolved that both creates and directs the actions and interactions of a group. A quorum is frequently considered indispensable to a valid religious act.

In and through the religious act the religious *group* is constituted. There is no religion that has not evolved a type of religious fellowship. In several other publications I have stressed the double relationship that characterizes the religious group in distinction from other types of groupings: first, the relation of its members—collectively and individually—to the *numen,* and second, the relation of the members of the group *toward each other.* While in personal experience the latter relationship may be met first, it is, ontologically, dependent upon the former, namely, the orientation to the numen. In another context we have said that the nature, intensity, duration, and organization of a religious group depends upon the way in which its members experience God, how they conceive of and communicate with Him, and how they experience fellowship, conceive of it, and practice it. More than other types of association, the religious group presents itself as a microcosm with its own laws, outlook on life, attitude, and atmosphere. Except for certain developments in the modern Western world, there has always been a consciousness of the numinous character inherent in the religious communion, in the *ecclesia,* the *qahal,* the *ummah,* or the *samgha.* Only where historical developments have led to a degeneration in the life of the fellowship, and hence to a weakening of this feeling, will there be a rationalistic or mystic or spiritualist protest against the actual manifestation, or against the very idea of a communion and community in religion. The numinous character of the fellowship, which might be reflected in myths or formulated in doctrine ("ecclesiology"), is not only, as some would assume, the result of its venerable age. It also results from the "power and glory" that it possesses because of its divine foundation. It is important to realize that there is this dimension to the notion of the religious community because the secularized understanding of many modern Westerners cannot conceive of it except in purely sociological terms.

The first important task for a student of religious groups will be, therefore, to do justice to the *self-interpretation* of a religious communion. How does it see its own nature in the light of the central religious experience that created and that sustains it? This question cannot be answered by taking into account only outward and measurable "behavior" and disregarding the meaning that concepts, attitudes, and acts are meant to convey. As over against this "intention" the actual performance in the past and in the present will have to be understood and judged. In what sense is the religious experience of a religious community genuine and fruitful? What is it that is revealed concerning the nature of Ultimate Reality? And how does it move man? How does it influence his attitude toward the world and the major spheres of activity within it? What does it mean in terms of his relation to his fellow men? Are there distinctions and qualifications? And upon what grounds are they made and justified? All this will tell us a great deal about a group, its prevailing spirit, and its fundamental attitudes. Religious communities vary not only with regard to the manner in which they apprehend the numen, that is, the content of the theoretical expression of their religious experience, but also in the degree of their religious fervor or intensity. The intensity of religious feeling and the urgency of the religious concern differ greatly from group to group.

As far as the relationship of the members of a religious group to each other is concerned, we might well expect to find a dimension of depth to which a nonreligious association will not—necessarily—aspire. In primitive religion a strong tie binds the members of a tribal cult together, and on the level of the great religions spiritual brotherhood surpasses physical ties between brothers. A "father or a mother in God," a "brother or sister in God" may be closer to us than our

physical parents and relatives. No stronger tie is possible between human beings than being related to each other in God.
It may consecrate the bonds of blood, of neighborhood, of
cooperation, and it may cut them. Next to blood relationship
and marriage—both with physical ties—the religious life has
given rise to the relation between *master and disciple,* perhaps
the profoundest and most fruitful relationship between men
even though there is no physical bond. It is easy to see how
in this cosmos of relationships and interrelationships an order
is necessary in which participation itself would insure a minimum of recognition and dignity but in which the higher
endowed would take precedence over the less endowed. In
accordance with the nature of the basic religious experience
the conception of the nature and function of members of the
community will vary. Dependent upon whether age or insight,
power or skill, attitude or a set of deeds is regarded as the
criterion for the possession of grace, a *spiritual order* will
become manifest which may or may not coincide with any
other competing order.

The use of the personal nouns in some languages is interesting in this regard. Where the normal way of address
may be a formal use of the second person plural, religious
language would favor the second person singular (intimacy).
The first person singular will often be circumscribed by expressions denoting humility while the first person plural, "we,"
serves to indicate, often in sharp opposition to the outside,
what the sociologist calls the *in-group.* In a genuine religious
community the satisfaction of forming a part of the group—
however insignificant—will be outweighed by the humble realization of the members' shortcomings. The presence of un-
mitigated pride, ambition, and hypocrisy indicates the lack of
genuineness in the character of the basic experience and of
those who stand for it. Genuineness and intensity of religious
experience is, as we saw, an even clearer indication of the
character and value of a religious group than size or structure.

The size of a group is important not just with regard to
quantitative measurement. As long as the group is small and
intimate enough for each member to know the other—a

condition that rarely survives the early stages—great intensity of feeling, great solidarity, and great activity will characterize the members. Where the size is larger but membership is not yet limited by such criteria as birth and locality, the character of the community will be different. What is left to spontaneity in the smaller unit must be organized here. Relations may be impersonal instead of intimate; individual initiative might be replaced by representative action. Here the process of crystallization may begin anew. This process gains special significance where the religious community is established on the basis of universality without any restriction or limitation. The history of all the major religions presents many examples of the formation of new vital centers or brotherhoods in which we may see renewed attempts at the realization of the ideal fellowship.

I have studied the integration of the religious group at some length in my *Sociology of Religion* (pp. 36ff.). We saw earlier that symbolic expressions may be regarded as a primary means by which the members of a religious communion are united. As far as the various forms of intellectual expression such as myth and doctrine are concerned, we may notice two different effects: they might well increase the feeling of solidarity of those bound by them, but they may also act divisively. Some religious groups prefer precise doctrinal statements in order to enhance the cohesion of their members, and they are only secondarily concerned with the effect of such regulation upon spontaneity. Other communities value latitude without being disturbed by the vagueness and atomism that may result from an exaggerated breadth.

With regard to the practical expression of religious experience we have noted already that common acts of devotion and of service provide an incomparable bond of union between the members of a cult group. To pray together is a token of the deepest spiritual communion. To join in a specific act of devotion may constitute a permanent association. A brotherhood develops out of the common veneration of a prophet or a saint among any number of people. The act of sacrifice may stand as an example for many other cultic acts, the performance of which has a socially integrating effect. "Festivals and pilgrimages," I have said in another context, "are outstanding occasions, for here we find a close interrelation between different cultic activities such as purifications, lustrations, prayer, vows, offerings, sacrifices, and processions all of which are of particular interest both to the historian and the sociologist of religion" (*Sociology of Religion*, p. 42).Thus, at all levels of social grouping—in the family or the house, in marriage or friendship, in the kinship or the regional group, in the village or the city, in a nation or in a specifically religious community—we observe a strengthening of cohesion. This strengthening illustrates the integrating function of a common religious experience.

But is there not another side to the picture? History tells us not only of the socially constructive but also of the destructive power of religion. Have not the closest ties of blood and friendship been destroyed in the name of religion? Especially the history of the universal religions seems to illustrate this contention. Indeed, in order to create a new and profound spiritual brotherhood, based on the principles enunciated by a new faith, old bonds have to be broken. This break of sociological ties becomes one of the marks of the willingness to begin a new life. ("To become a disciple of the Buddha means to leave parents and relatives, wife and child, home and property and all else, as flamingos leave their lakes" [The *rigatha;* see above, pp. 10, 18].) It is a cause for the sincerest rejoicing when those lost are found again in a new consecrated bond of union. But for those who cannot be reunited with their natural brothers and sisters and friends, the spiritual family of brethren and sisters is waiting. Even the apparently socially destructive forces of religion turn out to be creative and beneficial.

The religious group, which, as we saw earlier, is a microcosm, speaks its own language. It may use the words and phrases of the outside world to express experiences, thoughts, and feelings to which there is no analogy, or new terms and constructions may be coined to do justice to these experiences. New and unaccustomed ways of communication are sought and found. New symbols will arise. The outsider may or may not easily find access into a group thus integrated. Even where the participants do not desire to stress differences, these differences will make themselves felt in contacts with the "outside world."

It is very important to study the structure of religious groups. This structure is determined by two sets of factors, namely, those of a religious and those of an extrareligious nature. Spiritual gifts such as healing and teaching are examples of religious factors; age, social position, ethics, and background are qualifications of a nonreligious character. The pattern or structure might follow that of the natural order: where the family or the tribe or the people function as a cult group, the natural and the religious order are identical. Or the pattern might be absolutely independent, and either be kept at a minimum or developed maximally. In the latter case the structure of the religious group will at no point coincide with other orders such as the social, economic, or political. There will be considerable variations with regard to duration and to differentiation between religious groups. From the ad hoc, quickly gathered, and quickly dispersed audience to the solid and lasting institutions that have survived for millennia, we find more or less ephemeral, more or less tightly knit fellowships. And as to differentiation, the variety is equally great. Many, perhaps the majority of cult groups show little differentiation; some exhibit a high degree of it. There seem to be four major factors that make for differentiation within a religious community. The first is differentiation in function. Even within a small group comprising only a few members who are united by the bond of common religious experience, a certain degree of division of functions will exist. It will fall to the elders or the most experienced to lead in prayer or chant; some of the younger members may be charged with providing whatever is needed for sacrificial purposes. One will be a teacher, while another will serve as a deacon or deaconess. The enormously complex ritual of some of the higher religions presupposes an extreme degree of specialization on the part of those who function in these rites. In ancient Mexico and

Polynesia, in West Africa, Egypt, Rome, Babylon, and Israel, in Hinduism and Confucianism, in Mahāyāna Buddhism and in the Catholic forms of Christianity we have examples of differentiation in cultic functions as well as social differentiation. In another context (above, p. 107) I have pointed out that the degree of differentiation of functions in the religious group does not necessarily depend upon the general cultural level. We find in Southeast American Indian cults, in Shinto, or in modern Western sectarianism elaborate specialization, just as we meet with a minimum of it in the highest forms of group religious life. Kinds of functions differ from one another in a variety of ways; among the most basic are differences between permanent and temporary, personal and hereditary, and actual and honorary functions.

Second, there is, in religious groups, a differentiation according to charisma. Even the most egalitarian communities recognize a diversity of "gifts," which accounts for the differences in authority, prestige, and position within the community. Max Weber has spoken of hierarchies, and he has introduced into wider use the distinction between personal and official charisma. The highest conceivable charisma with which a person may be credited is constant and close communion with the "numen," the deity. Extraordinary powers can accrue to one so blessed, and there is no limit to what others may expect in demonstration of such powers. The esteem in which such a man or god may be held may express itself in a position of influence, of power, or of wealth or, inversely, in the complete absence of these qualities: weakness, poverty, and persecution. Next to this first type of primary charismatic, there is a derivative type: those who by some contact, possibly long and close, with the "friend of God" have acquired charisma, which places them in a category different from that of an ordinary member of the community: the apostles, companions, and first disciples of the great charismatics can be listed here.

The "gifts" of the charismatic may be of different kinds but will indicate a high degree of spiritual power. It may be insight into the divine mysteries, the nature of Ultimate Reality, and of the laws governing the existence of the cosmos, of society, and of individual lives; or the gift of restoring into wholeness broken physical or spiritual health; or the ability to develop, by teaching and in other ways, the hidden possibilities in one's fellow men, and to give direction and purpose to their lives. It may be physical strength or intellectual power, moral goodness, skill, or abnormal faculties. The possession of such charisma, sociologically seen, may have two effects: it may isolate its bearer to a greater or lesser degree, and it may become the focus of a process of social cystallization and thus serve to integrate.

A third factor making for differentiation within religious groups is the natural division according to age, sex, and descent. The young—as well as the old, though for different reasons—will be set somewhat apart and play, individually and collectively, a different role in the life of a religious community. (cf. on the religion of age groups Allport's *The Individual and His Religion*, chaps. 2 and 3). The preparatory stage during which the full privileges of membership are withheld ends with an initiation into full participation. Different groups of youth may be organized according to age (infants, young, older adolescents). In a body, a "senate," the aged may function as a "presbytery," as "elders"; but as individuals the old seer, prophet, teacher, and master will play an important role in the group, whether it be a natural group or specifically religious.

Men and women are often separated in the cultus or in certain functions while they may freely mix in other activities of a religious character. Women were excluded from the service of the Ara Maxima, men from the temple of the Bona Dea in ancient Rome. There are cult associations that exclude all except men or women at a specific age level. While in some religious communities only men may be religious functionaries, in others this role is reserved for women, and in still others both sexes are eligible for such service.

Differentiation according to descent might mean that racial qualifications are practiced according to which members of certain "races" are excluded from attending or fully partici-

pating in religious rites. Of this we know many examples in
Africa, Asia, Europe, and the Americas. It may also mean
that certain privileges with regard to the religious life and its
activities are limited to members of one or several special
racial groups. It is at this point that universal and tribal
(particular) faiths are most definitely at variance. Differentiation according to descent includes also distinctions made on
the basis of historical events such as conquest and war. Where
a group of people, by virtue of belonging to a political, cultural,
or ethnic unit, actual or fictitious, is barred from partial or
full participation in worship or from carrying out honorary
or other functions of a religious nature, there is differentiation
according to descent.

Fourth, religious communities may be differentiated according to status. This principle may be looked upon as a
combination of a number of factors that make for diversity.
The "democratic" notion of the equality of all believers is a
late product in the history of religions and, strictly speaking,
rarely if ever carried out in practice. Where there are no
differences based on the three criteria that I have already
discussed, distinctions from without or of a nonreligious character will make themselves felt. There are differences in property, in function in society at large, and in rank. Differentiation
within a religious community according to these factors, of
course, is more frequently than not "unofficial;" it exists de
facto rather than de jure. More often than not the wealthy
are accorded special privileges, the chief or the political leader
wields unwarranted influence, the nobleman or -woman and
other highly placed persons are deferred to, even though a
religious legitimation for such a distinction does not exist. Yet,
there are mythological and theological explanations in some
religious communities, especially in certain primitive Indo-
European societies, in India, and in Japan, which justify differences of status in the religious community. The difference
between legitimate and illegitimate distinctions of this kind is
very important for the development and history of cult fellowship (protests, reformations).

The actual structure of the religious group with which we have been concerned so far may be reflected in its constitution. This is a legal term, and it should be reserved for designating an organization prescribed and guaranteed by religious law. This is to say that in small religious communities and in those of a "pneumatic" character, there are usually few differences and there is little that can be called law. On the other hand, the constitutions regulating the life of the Christian Church in its various forms, of Judaism and Islam, Hinduism and Parsism, of Buddhism and Confucianism, were or are highly complex. Invariably the principles of the canonical law in all of these ecclesiastical bodies are derived from basic theological formulations of religious insights, and invariably there is a considerable margin for the interpretation of these principles. I have developed elsewhere the distinction between egalitarian and hierarchical organizations and suggested "minimum" and "maximum" types. Only within a constitution can differentiations according to function, charisma, natural factors, and status become legalized and sanctioned.

It may be that what existed de facto becomes de jure. There are also, however, examples of religious groups inside and outside Christianity that have adopted a strict constitution as soon as they have come into existence or shortly thereafter. However, the constitution of the major Catholic, Protestant, and sectarian Christian Churches, of the Jewish, Islamic and Parsi bodies, of the Buddhist and Jaina Samghas, and of Confucianism, are in each case the result of complex historical developments. The constitution regulates the duties and rights of the religious functionary (clergy) and of the laity, and the order of the former. It further regulates the forms of worship and of service. It defines the holy law, mediating principles and the application of these principles, and may include casuistry.

Elsewhere I have enumerated and analyzed some types of constitutions of religious groups (*Sociology of Religion*, Chapter 5). Natural as well as specifically religious communities may be ordered by such a constitution, for example, kinship or local cults, secret or mystery societies, brotherhoods, ecclesiastical bodies, monastic orders, or independent and sectarian groups. There will be regulations concerning the relationships between the community and the numen and between the various members (permanent and transitory relations), regulations that specify how the community is to be governed, the norms by which it is to exist, the representation of those ruled, discipline (admission and expulsion), material contributions, etcetera. Since there may be some latitude for regional and other differences, there will be a distinction between perennial and temporary provisions. Broadly speaking, the regulation of the relation of the whole institution to its government or leadership, of its parts to the whole (the individual congregation), and of the individual to the higher sociological and ecclesiastical units may be either more democratic or more authoritarian. According to the constitution of the group the various functions and orders in the culture are defined.

Just as fundamental as the problem of the communicability of religious experiences is the problem of religious authority. With a few exceptions—for example, skeptics, religious individualists, and anarchists—we are all inclined to agree that there is and must be authority in religious matters. (See W. Jaeger's statement in his *Theology of the Early Greek Philosophers,* p. 177: "The concept of *auctoritas* which is later to be of such decisive importance for the attitude of the Church in questions of faith, is entirely missing in Greek thought"). It seems preposterous to claim that everything should start *de novo* as if there had never been any communication between God and man. God has revealed himself to man, and the history of religion is the story of man's understanding and appropriation of this self-disclosure. "By these contacts with the unseen, the individual may become the 'organ' or 'mouthpiece' of the divine" (*Sociology of Religion*, p. 335). Elsewhere I have outlined a typology of the bearers of religious authority continuing the studies of Max Weber, Max Scheler, Rudolf Otto, F. Znaniecki, and others: founder, reformer, prophet, seer, magician, diviner, saint, priest, and *religiosus*. This typology indicates variations in the authority that personal or official charisma confers upon the *homo religiousus*. But not all claims to authority can be honored. All religions have faced the task of distinguishing between true and false prophets and between genuine and spurious saints. What are the criteria by which such distinctions can be made and with whom does the competence to make them rest? It has been all too true that the authority of one speaking in the name of religion has been taken to be self-authenticating. The vicious circle established between the claim and the demonstration of its validity on such grounds has been the curse of many a religious tradition in many a religious community. In fact, none has escaped it. And yet there is in the case of every individual claim the chance of weighing it in the light of the total revelation of the divine nature and character. If we were right (cf. above) in stating that truth can only be *one* and that ultimately the knowledge of truth must be unified, too, consistence and coherence with what has been revealed in the course of human history cannot count for nothing. "Each immediate religious experience must be set in relation with our total range of experience and thought; untested experience is not trustworthy" (E. S. Brightman, *A Philosophy of Realism,* p. 191). It can only be the depth of religious insight and truth that can guarantee the veracity and legitimacy of any claim made by a *homo religiosus,* by a group of those speaking in the name of religion, or by a religious institution. The question of how we may test authorities is also discussed in E. L. Wenger's interesting analysis of the problem of truth in religion (*Studies in History and Religion,* p. 177ff.): "The authority that man recognizes in religion," he says there, "is one who, in his character and manner of life, gives the impression of having insight into truths that ordinary man cannot fathom." He also stresses the necessity of seeing larger contexts: "The expert in religious truth must be one who has, implicitly or explicitly, a capacity to see the whole of life and to have a message adequate to it" (ibid., p. 178).

The question of motivation becomes of great importance if we want to assess the veracity of anyone claiming religious authority. Are the motives pure or mixed? If the latter, where does personal ambition or desire for power, wealth, or well-being begin and end? Since Freud, Jung, Pareto, and others have investigated the problems of the so-called subconscious mind, the study of personality has made great strides. I have become convinced that the relationship between conscious reasoning and the drives that propel it needs close scrutiny in every case where much depends on its character. It will always be difficult to analyze and to describe the *spirit* that prevails in a group united by common religious experience, a common faith, and common worship. An intensely religious group will always be a highly integrated group. The *solidarity* that characterizes the members both binds them together and sets them off over against outsiders. There is a wide gamut of "tokens" and signs by which the members of a given cult group can be identified, beginning with outward marks or emblems (such as painted or tattooed signs or patterns, lacerations, pieces of garment or vestment). These signs reveal a characteristic spirit. In some religious groups little value is placed upon the identification of members, and a greater or lesser degree of participation is not only tolerated but officially recognized. Other groups think of membership in strict terms. In this case admission—other than by inherited right—depends upon whether one fulfills definite obligations of various kinds. There are criteria for membership in good standing, and membership is voted or decided upon by a competent body or person. Discipline is enforced, and provisions for the exclusion of the unworthy are made. As a result, it is possible to make out who may—or may not—be considered to be a good Christian, Jew, Muslim, Parsi, Buddhist, Jain, or Confucian. There are, in each case, courses of action or attitudes that are considered, according to basic religious principles, or according to tradition or custom within a community of faith, as very specifically *not* in harmony or actually contrary to the spirit of the particular cult group. A great distance separates the infraction of a rule concerning dress, food, or participation in certain activities from violating basic moral ordinances by outspoken criminal acts. Within Jewish, Muslim, Hindu, Buddhist, and Christian theologies there have been discussions as to what constitutes a true believer and to what degree the actual community may be said to represent the ideal community. This ideal community may or may not be identified with a particular community of the past, for example, the mythical community of the beginning or the historical first circle or brotherhood. It may bear eschatological features (messianism in Judaism, Christianity, Islam, Hinduism, and Buddhism). In many religious communities certain mythical or historical figures are regarded as protoptypes of the true believer; frequently the founder or outstanding prophets and leaders play this paradigmatic role. The emulation of their virtues and attitudes becomes a guide to perfection. This ideal might be broken down still further, so that the exemplary man and the exemplary woman, the exemplary aged one or youth are recognized in persons of the most distant or most recent past (the "saint"). They may lend their names to the designation of a group of followers.

It remains for us to consider now the religious group in its relation to the world at large. So far I have concentrated on the cult community as a microcosm and studied it in relative isolation, but I did not intend to deny the existence and importance of such relationships. Again there is a wide range between the maximal identity of religion and other activities such as prevail in primitive societies and the tension we find existing on more advanced levels of cultural and religious development. Elsewhere, following Max Weber, we have suggested three basically different attitudes toward the world: a naively positive one, a negative one, and one critically positive. The first is illustrated by the outlook of the Veda or the Homeric epics, the second by the philosophy of Gnosticism or Buddhism, the third by the evaluation of the world in the monotheistic religions. Whatever the prevailing mood, the religious association takes precedence over all other forms of associating. Except in the modern Western world (cf. H. Schneider's *Religion in Twentieth Century America*), religious loyalty outranks any other loyalty. Certainly it does so in theory. In the West, we are now coming to understand that the gradual emancipation of one sphere of life after another from religion has had some extremely serious and pernicious consequences. To say this is not to endorse the policies and attitudes of religious institutions or their spokesmen, whether past or present, but to maintain the principle that religious values are either humanity's supreme values or they are not religious values at all. In different religious groups, different values provide religious values with the most serious competition: the values realized in economics, in sex, in art, in science, or in the state. Although some cult communities place no limitations on trade or commerce, others have severe restrictions. Some communities, far from being hostile toward sexual gratification, are fond of sexual symbolism and imagery; in other communities, the act of procreation and all that pertains to it are under heavy censure. Most religious groups expect the arts to contribute their share to the cultic expression of religious experience, but in some communities the arts are frowned upon and excluded from all forms of worship. Under the aegis of religious tradition the pursuit of knowledge is assiduously cultivated in most societies, but in some instances it has led to a sharp antagonism between religion and science. As far as political activity is concerned, a variety of typologically different attitudes toward the state as the highest form of societal organization can be traced. I have devoted a chapter to the comparative study of the relationship between religion and state (*Sociology of Religion,* chap. 7). All this means that associations for these or other purposes are differently evaluated on the basis of different religious experiences, and the relationship between cult groups and other associations will correspondingly differ. Everything is very simple in the case of the intimate religious community where practically all activities can be shared. In natural as well as specifically religious groups of this size a close integration of activities and associations exists under the inspiration of religion. Where differentiation and specialization have progressed, it is more difficult to prevent partial or total emancipation of economic, artistic, and erotic interests when a conflict of loyalties appears. In the case of a specifically religious group such conflicts are particularly frequent as their very emergence may represent a protest against certain political, economic, or moral conditions. Here sovereignty might actually clash with sovereignty, as was the case of feudal Western Christianity and feudal Japanese and Tibetan Buddhism, the religious might clash with the secular. There may also be friction or struggle between several religious groups competing within the same political realm. In developing certain basic religious institutions and principles, and applying them to typical situations and even concrete cases, mediating principles were formulated, as in the great systems of religious laws of Judaism, Islam, Hinduism, Confucianism, and the Catholic branches of Christianity. In many cases, such principles arrested the process of application at a given stage, producing a conflict between traditional religion and the continually developing feelings and attitudes of the people.

It is interesting to study comparatively the meaning and function which the notion of the religious community actually has for its members, especially in the case of great mass cults. In Judaism, despite the rather far-reaching differences between the orthodox, conservative, and liberal wings, and the existence of national variants, including pro- and anti-Zionists, there is a definite, overall consciousness among practically all Jews everywhere of *being one* (a *qahal,* or people), and this feeling is predominantly a religious feeling. Every congregation and every individual Jew will immediately feel that it, she, or he belongs to this great unit. Similarly in Hinduism there is a consciousness shared by hundreds of millions of followers of belonging to a community held together by the careful observances of the traditional rites and institutions, again despite the significant differences in doctrine, cult, and organization that distinguish Vaiṣṇavas (of different Sampradāyas), Śaivites and Śāktas, not to mention minor groups. It would be difficult to think that in any case the solidarity felt among the Hindus as a religious community could be broken by any other principle of grouping, even political. Less regionally bound than Hinduism, Islam, at least in the past, has been a brotherhood whose solidarity has superseded all other principles of association, only to be challenged in recent times by the claims of national loyalty. Very great geographical, ethnic, and cul-

tural variations and some important religious divisions (Sun-
nites; Shiites and their subdivisions, the four Madhabs; traditionalism; and Sufism) separate Muslims from each other;
yet, they all join in the consciousness of belonging to a great
brotherhood. A somewhat peculiar situation prevails with regard to Buddhism. No overall organization exists. Only in
some forms is there any higher unit beyond the individual
congregation. There is the important division into "vehicles"
with all that it means for the threefold expression in doctrine,
cult, and organization. There are the geographical, ethnic,
and cultural variations. Yet, a feeling for the unity of the
saṃgha does exist; and more than in the case of these previously
discussed religions, the individual Buddhist does "represent"
the ideal that integrates the *saṃgha*. As with the other world
religions, historical developments and the genius of the people
who profess them are reflected in the type and degree of
consciousness of solidarity in Christianity. Early in its history
divisions occurred on the basis of national, political, cultural,
and religious differences. The key term—*ecclesia*—was used
for the local congregation as well as for the total community
of the followers of Christ, his "body," the church. In the early
centuries various Oriental churches emerged; in the eleventh
century the great split into an Eastern and Western Church
occurred; and from the days of the Reformation a plurality
of bodies has existed with rivaling claims to represent the true
Christian communion. Besides ecclesiastical bodies, there were
denominations, independent groups, sects, and other communities, typologically differing from each other in the integration of their fellowship. The feeling of solidarity did not
extend clearly to the whole of the Christian brotherhood; each
of the major units into which it became divided received the
main part of its members' loyalty. Only half a century ago
did the so-called ecumenical movement in Protestantism begin
to gain ground; for centuries attempts in this direction had
been suspect and remained fruitless.

    Not only the most encompassing but also the smallest
manifestation of a religious community is instructive for comparing different religions. Christianity, both Catholicism and

Protestantism, has the congregation and the parish. Very recently illuminating studies of the sociology of the Catholic parish in France and the United States have appeared. P. F. Fichter, the author of *The Southern Parish,* has rightly said that a systematic understanding of the role of Catholicism in modern society requires us to study not only its values and meanings but more especially the "vehicles" employed to activate them and the agents who believe in these values and employ these "vehicles." The parish is "the church in miniature." Is the population of a parish religiously *homogeneous?* The answer is no: there are in this case (1) non-Catholics; (2) dormant and former Catholics; (3) actual parishioners. And what are the standards by which the degree of activity can be estimated? Fichter enumerates the following: religious vocations coming from the parish, attendance at Mass, sacraments, week-day devotions, parochial activities, parish schools, number of converts, number of juvenile delinquents, mixed marriages, and size of families. In answering these questions, we begin to understand that there is great variety in the degree of activity and hence in the nature of membership in a parish.

III

Are the categories developed in the preceding section applicable to the American scene? I believe that they are. Without any prejudice all existing religious communities—and their variety is great—can be subsumed under the title of religious groups. In a recent appraisal of religion in twentieth century America, Schneider suggests a distinction between movements and bodies, the former dynamic, the latter static organizations. "A religious body," he says, "is a stable institution with a heritage which it cherishes, a government which gives organized expression to its faith, and a body of members whose duties and values are generally recognized." "Most movements," he continues, "culminate in bodies, as most faiths become creeds. A movement is endangered when it does not create a body and a body is endangered when it ceases to

move" (H. W. Schneider, *Religion in Twentieth Century America,*
p. 22).

I have tried to replace the old dichotomy of churches and
sects by a trichotomy. I divide American religious groups into
ecclesiastical bodies, denominations, and sects. Religious communities as different as the Roman Catholic Church and the
Church of the Latter-Day Saints are ecclesiastical bodies. They
are characterized by a claim to authority, authoritatively defined doctrines, sacraments, and orders. Ecclesiastical bodies
on the American scene may be supranational or more clearly
nationally oriented: the Roman Catholic Church and the Mormon Church illustrate the first, the Scandinavian and German
Lutheran churches the latter group.

The second type of religious community was first described
by J. M. de Jong, "The Denomination as the American Church
Form," *Nieuw Theologisch Tijdschrift* 27 (1938):347–388, as
denominations and declared to be *the* American church form.
H. R. Niebuhr analyzed its social sources. Sidney Mead has
developed this notion further. The denomination is distinguished from the ecclesiastical body through the principle of
voluntary association and by congregational organization, and
from the sect by size, prevailing mood, and "democratic"
leadership. The Congregationalists, Baptists, Methodists, and
Unitarians are denominations in this sense. Although there is
an unmistakable tendency toward denominationalism in all
American religious communities, and although denominations
have dominated the cultural history of America, I feel it is
not quite correct to call the denomination *the* American church
form. Significant contributions have also been made by both
ecclesiastical bodies and sects, as they will continue to do in
the future. The denomination, due to a certain lack of definite
structure, is on the defensive today on both fronts. I think
one of the reasons for the weakness of denominations and the
relative vitality of ecclesiastical bodies and sects is that history
is often a denomination's most important *raison d'être,* while
theology plays a secondary role. But theology is central in
both churches and sects. It is not impossible that the realign-
ment in American Protestantism that is now taking place will

disregard historical and sociological lines and follow a more theological or religious pattern. If it does so, it will reverse the trend of Pietism, Revivalism, and other similar movements, but it will follow them in their indifference toward denominationalism (cf. World Council of Churches, Commission on Faith and Order, *The Nature of the Church,* 1952).

The third type of community is the sect in the sense in which European scholars such as Ernst Troeltsch have used this term. The sect tends to be small in size. Admission to a sect is conditioned and hence limited: a rigid exclusiveness characterizes this type of religious grouping. It stands for *protest,* protest against the latitudinarianism of both ecclesiastical bodies and denominations. While it shares with the former an insistence on the necessity of well-defined and rigidly adhered-to principles, strictly conceived authority, and discipline, it shares with denominationalism an opposition to traditionalism in principle and, empirically, to definite historical developments in doctrinal, practical, or social expressions. There is usually in sectarianism a special emphasis upon charismatic leadership. The Shakers, Jehovah's Witnesses, and the Bahai are instances of American sects, while the Quakers, Disciples, Brethren, Christian Scientists, Swedenborgians, the Nazarenes, and possibly the Mennonites represent sects in the process of becoming denominations. Though sects usually transcend national and racial lines, some are so limited by choice or by force, such as the black sectarian groups studied by St. Clair Drake, Raymond J. Jones, and Arthur H. Fauset. A peculiar phenomenon are the sects connected with Eastern (Oriental) religions, such as the Bahai, Vedānta, Theosophy, and others. A classification of sects could be suggested on psychological, sociological, and theological grounds, but as yet not much satisfactory work has been done. It is here that the limitation of a purely sociological approach becomes obvious. While two or more groups may present very similar pictures as far as the prevailing mood and the sociological structure are concerned, the theologies of these groups may be worlds apart (Adventist-Holiness-Pentecostal groups). While the character of certain movements and groups is to a large extent defined by sociological criteria, such as the earlier so-called Frontier religion or now the Buchmean (Oxford group) Movement, which Allan Eister has recently analyzed in his book *Drawing Room Conversion,* we find that the more definitely a religious group is a religious group—as distinct from an economic, political, or cultural association—the more important, both for members of the group and students of it, will become its worship and its theology. I am inclined to regard a healthy tension between religion and cultural environment as a surer sign of religious vitality than an "adjustment" to the cultural scene, such as Professor Schneider seems to advocate. One word may be added on the so-called *Healing* groups, denominational and sectarian. Here the theological criterion is especially important. Such a group is religiously relevant only to the extent that a spiritual good rather than physical good (health, well-being) is at the center of the aspirations of its members. In the same sense the theological criterion helps us to distinguish an economic or political association from a religious grouping.

May I close with a personal remark? It seems to me that the current general statements made by historians, literary historians, and sociologists about American civilization often do not do justice to the fact that a considerable part of the American ethos is still, though less than in earlier periods of American history, expressed in religious commitment and its sociological expression. Church, denomination, and sect—each type of religious community and, within each, the different religious ideologies, practices, and covenants exhibit the genius of the civilization we call American.

ON TEACHING HISTORY OF RELIGIONS

THE 60TH BIRTHDAY of the great Dutch historian of religion whom this volume is to honour seems a suitable occasion to reflect upon the most adequate and effective way to *teach* the subject to which he has made such outstanding contributions. There is, of course, not *one* way or *one* method which, once developed, could be handed down from one generation of teachers to the other. The approach will have to be adapted to the special needs and demands of each successive generation. The motivation which led the students of, say, 1880 to take up the study of the history of religions was not the same as that causing novices to investigate it around 1900 or 1920. That is to say that not only the incentives to the study of the history of religions have varied in the last century—the first of its existence as "Wissenschaft"—but that ideas as to the aim and scope, the nature and the method of this discipline also have been changing. The history of studies in our fields has been competently traced by E. Lehmann, E. Hardy, Jordan, H. Pinard de la Boullaye and G. Mensching, but these efforts cover only the first three periods since Max Mueller established the comparative study of religion as an academic discipline, his own endeavours marking the *first* epoch, those of his immediate successors (C. P. Tiele) the *second,* the "religions-geschichtliche Schule" the *third.* I think it is possible to discern the beginnings of a fourth period in some works published since the first world war. Though R. Reitzenstein and R. Otto, W. Bousset and N. Söderblom were contemporaries, it seems to this writer that with Söderblom and especially with R. Otto a new phase in the development of our studies began. One of the exponents and leaders of this new "school" has been G. van der Leeuw.

During the first period which was marked by the somewhat sensational rise of "comparative" studies, the interest which prompted people to enter this field was, besides philological inclinations, the fascination of the exotic—a heritage from the romantics—to which were added during the second epoch folkloristic, archaeological and philosophical interests. While Max Müller's and Tiele's views of religion were determined by the teachings of German idealistic philosophy and its spec-ulative interpretation of Christian theology, these influences had greatly diminished with the advent of the third generation. The latter concentrated upon historical and philological tasks and showed, generally speaking, not much interest in nor-mative and systematic questions. The relativistic temper dom-inated. Theology was to be replaced by history of religions. Laymen and scholars were intrigued by the search for "par-allels" and environmental factors by which the rise and de-velopment of Christianity could be "explained." A great change came with the first post-war period. The generation which filled the auditoria in the early twenties of this century was not satisfied to hear what *had been* and what *could be* believed, but asked what it *ought* to believe. Systematic ("dogmatic") theology attracted many. Philosophy, hitherto preoccupied with epistemological and historical research seemed to promise new answers to "weltanschauliche" questions. The transition may be indicated by the names of Rickert and Husserl for the older, Scheler and Heidegger for the younger generation, with Dilthey and Troeltsch reflecting the change within the development of their own thought. Even while the tremendous harvest which a century of historically oriented scholarship had made possible was being gathered, the crisis of historism, which Troeltsch was the first to analyze on a monumental scale, became manifest.

Soon voices were heard which advocated the elimination of the superfluous "ballast" which the painstaking work of philologists, archaeologists, anthropologists, orientalists, and historians had accumulated, in favour of a simplified "credo," spontaneously formulated or derived from tradition to the exclusion of everything else. What is the use of history of religions? they ask. Attacks such as these often serve good purposes. They force a reconsideration and reconception of the nature, function and method of the discipline thus challenged. The *fourth* period witnesses numerous attempts to answer these questions though it cannot be denied that in some quarters little has changed in the pursuit of studies in our field since the turn of the century. This is not the place to examine critically the programs which have been suggested or the nature of the relationship of our own work to that in other fields. (Cf. my article on *The Place of the History of Religions in the Study of Theology* in the Journal of Religion, 1948.)

However, some *basic points* which are playing a part in this discussion need mentioning. It has been said that relativism is the inevitable consequence of a study of non-Christian religions. This impression was caused by the exaggerated enthusiasm of some representatives of the "religionsgeschichtliche Schule," voiced in a period in which the ultraliberal orientation of many Protestant theologians had weakened the religious conviction of many Christians. To-day we see that, far from endangering a well-grounded faith, Christian or otherwise, an acquaintance with other religions has a beneficial influence. First, it helps to overcome the fanaticism, narrowness and provincialism for which there is no room in the One World in which we have to live with others. Furthermore, a deepened understanding of certain elements in our own faith is frequently the result of studies in myths and forms of worship, and certain neglected emphases in our own teachings

and practices can be corrected. It is significant that inter-
preters, both of the Old and the New Testaments, have been
able to determine much more clearly and precisely the "Ei-
genart" of these documents and their views of God, world,
and men on the basis of studies in the religions of the ancient
Near East than could be done before the discoveries of the
nineteenth and twentieth centuries. (Cf. the recent *Symposium
on the Intellectual Adventure of Man*, Chicago, 1946 and R.
Bultmann, *Das Urchristentum im Rahmen der antiken Religionen*,
Basel, 1949.)

But there are other objections to the work of the historian
of religions. He chases a chimera, so it is said, because even
if it should be deemed desirable, it is not *possible* to penetrate
beyond the amassing of facts and data, into the "secrets" of
primitive or oriental religions. Thinking and feeling of the
peoples of so distant times and places are too different from
our own, it is argued, to allow a real understanding. One has
to be a member of a Buddhist samgha to understand Buddhism.
A real hermeneutical problem is raised with this objection,
but one to which there is a solution. First of all it has to be
said that, even if a real understanding should be impossible,
a good acquaintance with the teachings and practices of a
religious group already marks a great step beyond the prejudices born of ignorance which have so frequently tended to
poison the relations between members of different religious
communities. It is, moreover, the presupposition for successful
missionary work. But actually the situation is not as hopeless
as sceptics are wont to believe. There are degrees of understanding. (cf. J. Wach, *Das Verstehen*, Tübingen, 1926–32).
What is meant by "membership" in the samgha? Religious
groups are not—or certainly not in all cases are they—"clubs"
in which membership depends on the regular payment of dues
and similar external marks. The more it is the *spirit* which
forms the "marks" of "belonging," the less important becomes
the sociological factor. It could be asked if Snouck Hurgronje
or Louis Massignon have understood Islam less than an ignorant villager of the Dutch East Indies or of Northern Africa.
"Knowledge" in the sense of acquaintance with data, of course,

is not enough. An "affinity" which is difficult to analyze is necessary to enter into and comprehend the relationship between the data which represent the structure of a cult. Moreover, the "ethos" which prevails in a religious community has to be sensed, a process in which careful induction and sympathetic intuition have to be combined. The enormous progress which has been made in the understanding of foreign religions in the past century and a half proves that even if a total comprehension should be unobtainable a great deal of insight into their nature can be won.

There is, at least, one more doubt in the minds of those who are disinclined or reluctant to admit that some good can come out of the study of the history of religions. Some would question the identity and unity of the far-flung studies which together make up the work in our field. This unity is, indeed, difficult to conceive as long as only single data are seen—be they philological, archaeological, anthropological, historical or sociological. In order to relate these data and to interpret them as expressions of religious experiences, some notions of the *nature* of this *experience* are necessary. In other words the narrowly historical quest has to be supplemented by a systematic (phenomenological) one.

It is not possible in this context to develop a theory of religious experience and of its theoretical, practical and sociological expressions. Suffice it to say with regard to the special topic of this paper that certain *requirements* for teaching the history of religions to-day follow from the brief analysis of the situation which we have essayed here.

1. Instruction in our field must be *integral*. The student is entitled to expect some orientation as to the purpose which the accumulation of facts throughout his apprenticeship is meant to serve. If he does not ask fundamental questions as to the meaning of his pursuits by himself, he must be made to see the larger contexts in which each detail, small or important, can and must be placed to become meaningful. The interrelationship of all forms of knowledge must become just as visible as the functional unity of life and of civilization.

2. Instruction in our field must be *competent*. No enthusiasm or loyalty can be allowed to replace thorough training and discipline, especially in the methods of philological and historical research. The student must be led to the sources. However, this is only one part of the equipment. The other consists in an acquaintance with the nature of religious experience, an acquaintance which, after all, is the indispensable prerequisite for the work of the historian of religion.

3. Instruction in our field can be fruitful only if it is dictated by an *existential* concern. The study of religion presupposes congeniality. The general hermeneutical rule that some likeness is necessary for all understanding has to be applied to the special case. There is nothing more painful than the helpless attempt at the interpretation of religious documents or monuments by one who does not know what "awe" is or to whom these testimonies to man's search for communion with ultimate reality are just the dead records of the experience of "sick-minded" or backward people.

4. Instruction in our field must be *selective*. The enormous amount of material accumulated during the last century and a half of careful research can not and should not be "covered" in our teaching. Choices have to be made. The typological method will prove very useful in the attempt to include a variety of *representative* forms of expressions of religious experience to the student. Though a very intimate knowledge of one or the other religion based on thorough knowledge of the sources is the "admission-ticket" to the workroom of the historian of religions, provincialism and the false perspective resulting from it are dangers which he can only avoid by reference to and comparison with typologically different expressions of religious experience.

5. Instruction in our field must be *balanced*. The history of our discipline is replete with examples of leading scholars and schools preoccupied with one or the other form of expression of religious experience: theoretical or practical, myth or cultus, rational or mystical piety, individual or collective religion. It is easily understandable that, because one or the other form of expression will show a greater development

within one historical religion, the "expert" in *these* religions will tend to absolutize the structure of this form of devotion. Here the historian must look to the phenomenologist (in van der Leeuw's sense) or to the student of systematic Religionswissenschaft for help.

6. Instruction in our field must be *imaginative*. This is not to say that we are advocating a flight away from the facts into the realm of the fantastic but rather a reminder to the teacher to be aware of the gap that has to be constantly bridged between the ways of thinking and feeling of our own age and climate and those of peoples removed from us in space and time. Psychology, anthropology and sociology will be of great assistance here, the more so because recent developments in these fields, tending toward integration of these intimately related pursuits, promise the creation of a *study of man* to which the investigation of his religious life has to add an important, nay a decisive dimension.

Finally, a practical problem to which attention has to be given is that of *levels of instruction*. Different conditions prevailing in different countries make different solutions necessary. Nearly all European teaching is graduate instruction while in the United States the division between undergraduate and graduate work is marked. In Europe the academic teacher is expected to do both research *and* teaching, and there can be no doubt that this combination is very healthy and has good effects on the quality of both research and instruction. The same demand is made in the United States for the teacher on the graduate level but not necessarily for those entrusted with the teaching of undergraduates. Whereas previously the existing law prevented any instruction in religion at least in State colleges, recently more and more institutions of higher learning have begun to introduce such courses. In most cases some teaching in the Bible, in Christian ethics and (or) in comparative religion has been instituted. Because in different States of the Union and in different institutions different courses have been adapted and the whole development is of rather recent origin, it is, as yet, not possible to get a clear over-all picture of the situation. Some of the programs provide courses dealing with the religious "Umwelt" of the Bible; general surveys of primitive, higher and highest religions; typological treatment of varieties of religious experience; presentation of the major living world religions, of the life and teaching of outstanding religious leaders, etcetera. An added difficulty is the difference in the denominational background of the students in many institutions of higher learning in the United States. The less the teacher in the field can be expected to do research himself, the more important becomes the question of adequate text-books. It is characteristic of the difficulties prevailing that though the number of manuals of the history of religions is legion, the main American standardwork, G. F. Moore's treatise, is over 25 years old and has been reprinted only recently. French, German, Dutch, Scandinavian, and Swiss handbooks are much more up to date. Yet, in most of these manuals little more than a juxtaposition of treatments of different non-Christian religions is to be found. The task of tracing "developments," of discerning types of structure and attitudes, of raising the problem of value and truth is left to the philosopher. Here some integration is necessary; fundamental epistemological and even metaphysical problems will have to be introduced to overcome the atomization of knowledge, the heritage of the positivistic age.

Even the most cursory introductory course must reflect some of the theological, philosophical, anthropological and sociological discussions which are carried on to-day. It is well-known that introductory courses are especially difficult to teach, and those in our field are no exception to this rule. They are best entrusted to the most experienced, not to the least experienced of the faculty. The ideal procedure would be to continue the introductory course by a three-term sequence, the first of which would be given over to a presentation of so-called primitive religions, the second and third dedicated to the religions of the West and of the East, or of the higher and highest (world) religions respectively. But if enough time is not available, a basic course could be worked out on a typological basis in which one primitive cult, one of the ancient religions of the Near East and the two great competitors of

Christianity—Islam and Buddhism—could be dealt with. Added courses or alternatives would treat great religious leaders or some basic idea, institution or phenomenon on a comparative basis. All these topics would be of interest to the student who desires a general education, whatever his subject of concentration. (This includes students in the sciences, too.)

For those specializing in our field and working toward a degree, especially a higher degree, the situation is, of course, different. Here alternative programs will have to be provided which must do justice to the special schooling and interests of candidates, e.g. philological, theological or philosophical training. There will have to be a common core of work, of course, but opportunities must be provided and requirements formulated so as to allow and to foster necessary and fruitful specialization. Whereas no special linguistic preparation will be expected of the undergraduate desiring some orientation in the field, the graduate student or anyone desirous to specialize in the study of the history of religions, even if he does not intend to do research himself, but wants to devote himself to teaching on a middle or higher level, must prove competence in dealing with the material. It will depend again upon the nature of his work, whether this competence should be merely passive (that is, consisting in the ability to check a translation etc.) or active (that is, enabling him to do creative research-work himself). Again it ought to be said that linguistic preparation is just one presupposition. For a competent handling of subjects which pertain to the domain of psychology, sociology of religion etc., a solid grounding in methodology and, generally, an acquaintance with the results of scholarship in the respective field has to be expected. It is, after all, a significant fact that some of the major contributions to the study of the history of religions has been made and still is being made by scholars who cannot be called "specialists" in our field. To sum up: it is not just a question of extending the limits of what is to be known and assimilated, but of realizing that, in order to focus the subject matter of our studies correctly, we have to reconceive its nature in the light of the best of *all* available thought and information.

In this respect G. van der Leeuw has set an example for which his contemporaries owe him much gratitude.

ON UNDERSTANDING

ALBERT SCHWEITZER is a master of understanding. Without a great natural talent—or shall we say genius—no amount of acquired skill and knowledge would have enabled him to interpret so profoundly and comprehensively as he has done personalities of the past, distant periods and peoples, great religious documents and works of art, the thoughts, feelings, and emotions of human beings from the standpoint of a theologian, an artist and a physician. *Interpres non fit sed nascitur.* [An interpreter is not made but born.] Yet, like all masters of a craft, he never relied on the inspiration of his genius but perfected his talents consistently and methodically by experience and study over a long period of years. His understanding, moreover, has proved to be deep and fruitful, because it is the result not only of a great and inclusive mind, but of an equally great and cultivated heart. A brief analysis of the nature of understanding, which he possesses to such an eminent degree, shall be our contribution in his honor.

All theories of understanding which try to analyze its nature and the stages of its development will have to begin with a concept of existence, and this means, implicitly if not explicitly, with a metaphysical decision. As I see it, there exist three possibilities which I should like to call the materialistic, the psychophysical and the spiritual interpretations of existence.

The materialistic conception explains the development and differentiation of the spiritual and psychic processes by evolution of matter. Its specific crucial problem is the immediate understanding of the minds of others.

The psychophysical conception admits that there is a mental existence apart from matter, so that it is possible for a man to share in the mental life of his fellows.

The spiritual interpretation, like the materialistic, assumes the unity of all existence, but in a different sense. Here the basis of understanding lies in the continuity of mental life. Three theories of understanding are based on this idea:

1. The religious concept of spiritual communion, that is, communion in the Holy Spirit;
2. Hegel's secularized theory of the unity of spirit; and
3. Nietzsche's modern biologistic philosophy of life, with its idea of the unity of all life. Because we share the same spirit, mind or life, we may be able to understand what is related to us in substance *"Wie kann ein Mensch Sinn für etwas haben, wenn er nicht den Keim davon in sich trägt?"* (Novalis) ("How can a man understand anything, if he does not carry the germ of it within himself?")

I think there must be some truth in the idea expressed by Plato and accepted by Goethe in its Neo-Platonic form: *"Wär' nicht das Auge sonnenhaft, die Sonne könnt es nie erblicken."* ("Were not the eye akin to the sun, it could never perceive the sun.") The religious flavor of this philosophy may be recognized in Malebranche's version: *"Nous voyons toutes choses en Dieu,"* which Ernst Troeltsch has recently taken over into his epistemology. To the extent that we are part of the divine creation do we see it in its true nature. Thus we obtain the hermeneutic principle that we cannot understand what is wholly different from ourselves. If we were also to say that we cannot understand what is wholly *like* ourselves, we would have to assume that understanding can apply only to an intermediate field, lying between what is wholly similar and what is wholly dissimilar to our nature. The wholly similar cannot be understood, because all understanding requires a certain *detachment* of the subject from the object.

We must now discuss whether we can understand equally well everything in which we participate. It is obviously impossible to understand life as a whole, either in its infinitely varied productivity, or in its totality, which makes it more than the sum of all individuals, their experience and their creations.

The same is the case with history in its most general aspect. We may attribute meaning to history, but such an interpretation can be nothing but a subjective evaluation, an *eisegesis*, not an *exegesis*.

It is quite a different matter when we turn to particular phases of life, to specific experiences, to individual emotions and thoughts, to the history of particular cultures, periods, events and phenomena. They have a definite meaning, which we can understand and interpret objectively, provided the necessary subjective presuppositions are fulfilled.

Facts, and groups of facts, may be of two kinds: they may either arise in subjective experience only or manifest themselves objectively in expressions of that experience. There are many different stages and types of expression; beginning with the transitory expression of psychic life in facial expression, they lead up to gestures and eventually to signs. In the third stage we find a certain independence of expression from the subjective psychic experience. A signal has a special meaning, which can be understood, but which can also be misinterpreted, because it is relatively independent of the intention of the person who makes it. If someone is waving to me with his hand, I—and perhaps other persons—may interpret that sign to mean that I should go away, whereas he might want me to come toward him. His expression, the signal, is ambiguous. We see that a signal may have a meaning which may be interpreted independent of or even contrary to the subjective intention; therefore, we have to reckon with two possibilities: a subjective and an objective interpretation of expression.

The next stage of objectification is realized when the meaning is inherent in an expression, communicated to us through a medium: sounds, words, and phrases, for instance, may be understood in a subjective and in an objective sense; each might have a distinct meaning. The analysis of the understanding of the composition of words and phrases, which had been first outlined most brilliantly by Wilhelm von Humboldt, is the task of philology, one of the fields in which a theory of interpretation has developed. The others are theology, with its theory of the interpretation of sacred writings, and jurisprudence with its theory of the interpretation of laws.

The third stage of objectification is represented by personal *documents*, which might be of monumental or literary character. Letters are an interesting example; they contain subjective expression with an objective meaning. Now I can interpret the meaning of a letter without regard to the subjective life of the writer. I may do it rightly or wrongly. To be sure that I have the right interpretation of it, that I have really understood it as it wanted to be understood, I must see it in its subjective context. In this respect, Feuerbach once said that letters are aphorisms cut from their context in life. So we see that we are led from the interpretation of a special configuration to more and more extended subjective and objective contexts from which the original object takes its color: the whole correspondence, the character and life of its author.

So far we have dealt with types of expression of psychic experience which are rather closely related to the subjective experience from which they originate. The maximum of objectification, independent of subjective life, is reached in works to which we can do justice without reference to their originator, such as historical documents, normative (legal or religious) writings, and works of art.

Within the realm of artistic creation we see differences of degree in this respect. The development from spontaneous gestures to the artistic dance and to the drama shows that expression is more or less bound to the personality of the actor or actress, while painting and architecture represent expression of a less personal character, their mediums being tangible and material. Music again is peculiar in this respect: the meaning of a musical composition is conveyed through sound, the subtlest vibrations of matter, and is relatively independent of the personality of its author. How complicated the problems of musical hermeneutics are, we may see from the following example, taken from my book, *Das Verstehen*. In the opera *Orpheus and Euridice* Gluck composed a special melodic line for the words: "Oh, I have lost her, and it is my greatest sorrow," and afterwards replaced these words with: "Oh, I have gained her, and it is my greatest joy," without changing the music. This illustrates the flexibility of music as a medium of conveying meaning.

So, in all understanding of more or less objectified expression which is to succeed in its intention, two factors combine: the subjective interpretation, which intends to make sure the psychological meaning of an expression by relating it to its author, and the objective interpretation, which takes it as an entity in itself and tries to unfold its meaning. The objective exegesis consists of three different procedures: the technical interpretation, analysis of the material or elements of expression (sounds, letters, colors); the generic interpretation, asking for the genre or *genos,* type or form of work; the historical and sociological interpretation, which attempts to elucidate the socio-historical background and the development of the phenomenon. None of these viewpoints should be unduly stressed at the expense of others if the aim is an integral understanding.

Michelangelo's famous paintings, "The Creation of Man," may serve as an example of highly objectified artistic expression. Understanding means, in this case, to be able to answer the questions: 1) What is to be seen? The answer is: a young man, lying on the ground, and an old man, gliding, as it were, from the air toward him; and 2) What does it signify? This question is not identical with the psychological inquiry, "What did the artist intend to express?" Rather, it refers to the objective meaning of this painting, which we may identify as the same or another than the artist intended to express. The answer is: the Lord, creating Adam, the first man.

In trying to illuminate the background, we must relate the painting to three different contexts. The first, the historical and sociological, interpretation, gives it a place in the history of art, of artists, of culture and of society. The second, or generic interpretation, analyses it according to its species and its technical character. The third, the documentary interpretation, places the work in a larger context of meaning, which might possibly be beyond the horizon of its creator; it illustrates the philosopher's shrewd remark, "The artist is ever wiser than he is." Here the success of hermeneutics lies in understanding the work of the author better than he himself did.

With this last type of interpretation we have already passed not only to inference, but also to *appreciation* and *application* of the meaning of the objectification of experience, and it is a problem whether this appreciation or application is a part of the process of understanding proper.

For instance, in the interpretation of art, interpretation, and appreciation or evaluation are closely connected, more so than in the interpretation of laws. And in the interpretation of religion, it is doubtful whether the meaning of a religious message can be understood without any reference to its hortatory character. That is how the early Protestant theologians conceive of understanding: *Primum perceptio, deinde cogitatio de illa percepta notitia in praxim, tertio velle, quarto perficere.* [First one perceives; then one reflects on what has been perceived with a view to action; then one wills; and finally one acts to carry out one's volition.]

Presuppositions, Conditions, and Limitations of Understanding

We have now to consider which subjective and objective presuppositions are necessary for adequate understanding and what the limitations of understanding itself are. We have already found that understanding aims at bringing into focus the unknown as an intermediate field between the entirely foreign and the perfectly familiar. Though we cannot say we understand the lower organisms, we succeed in interpreting the meaning of the gestures and sounds made by animals. Scheler has defined the dividing line between man and animals by attributing to man *Geist,* the ability to reflect on his own nature and to become a moral being, capable of renunciation and self-sacrifice. I would prefer to draw the line between those beings which are and those which are not able to create permanent expressions for their internal experience, which may be understood independently of subjective life. Therefore, we may say that understanding in a technical sense is limited to the realm of human life and human creations.

Why is it difficult for us at times to understand our fellow men and the expression of their experience? First, because we are—each of us—the complicated and highly individual result of slow development from an original germ. The second thing to remember is that the understanding subject does not live in a vacuum; he is conditioned in many ways by his environment. Our understanding, therefore, is necessarily limited, first, by what we are personally, and secondly, by the conditions under which we exist. Thus we can say that the chances for understanding persons and things are in some respects worse and in others better than some epistomologists think.

Two extreme attitudes, however, must be avoided: a naive realism, which hopes to grasp the object "as it is," and a subjectivistic skepticism, which dissolves the object into relations. Not relativism, but relationism, should be the motto of all sound hermeneutics.

The understanding of individuality is the basic problem of hermeneutics. *"In der Individualität liegt das Geheimnis alles Daseins"* [Individuality contains the secret of all existence], said Humboldt, and Dilthey agrees with him: *"Individuum est ineffabile."* That means that individuality is not only inexpressible but also incomprehensible. In the different methods of investigation of personality, however, some methods have been developed to solve this mystery. Without doubt the theory of types is suitable in serving the understanding of personality, although exaggeration may be dangerous and lead to fantastic conclusions. If we want to understand the actions and reactions of a person, we use categories like "the hero," "the coward," "the miser," "the lover," to make his motivation and scale of values plausible to us. Dilthey has demonstrated the importance of types of human character for the understanding of personalities in literature in his thesis on Shakespeare. History and poetry present additional difficulties for an understanding. The personalities in dramatic poetry, for instance, are seen through the medium of the poet. Thus we must differentiate between the "objective" meaning and the highly personalized interpretation which the actor may give to a particular role and to individual lines in attempting to convey the specific intentions of the dramatist.

What we do in daily life, the historian practices in his study in viewing historic personalities in the light of characterological types. Furthermore, history is always related through some sources. Sometimes an actual witness describes the events and the personalities figuring in them; sometimes again we have more than one source through which we must understand historical events and personalities. Sometimes the understanding of a character presents special difficulties, particularly if we have very few objective expressions as material. If we face a person, we may interpret his speech by examining the caliber of his voice, the expression of his eyes, and his gestures, so that we are able to discern clearly whether his words are straightforward, or ironical, or ambiguous. Since all literal and historical analysis misses this advantage, the student must combine very carefully as much material as he can collect on his subject.

After these remarks on the objective difficulties of understanding, we may consider briefly its subjective conditions, which are the presuppositions for the understanding of the not entirely foreign and the not perfectly familiar. He who wants to understand appears to be confined within the magic circle of his personality, yet it is not entirely so. I would like again to quote an example from the history of religion. The historian of religion deals with exotic, ecstatic and primitive cults, all of them more or less foreign to his mind and his soul, still more to his personal experience. He has never participated in complicated rites; he has never taken part in ecstatic sessions or performances. He knows animals—totems in the primitive language—only as they occur around the house or at the zoo. Nevertheless, there exists some means of breaking the magic circle of these limitations. All of us are able to enlarge the limits of our empiric personality: the first means is by availing ourselves of the immeasurable treasure of research and the arts, which enables us, through knowledge and comparison, to gain analogies for the phenomena which we wish to understand. A great modern philosopher defines art as an organ for the understanding of life. All natural sciences and the humanities make their contributions to the enlargement of the empiric self.

The second way is indicated by the words of Goethe: "*In jedem Menschen liegen alle Formen des Menschlichen.*" ("In every man all forms of human character are potentially present.") Goethe felt, when told about a crime, that he would have been capable of committing it himself. Modern students have emphasized the fact that our conscious life does not complete the entire circle of our personality. I refer to a very interesting report of Eduard Spranger in the transactions of the "Berliner Akademie der Wissenschaften" (1930): "Über die Schichten des Wirklichkeitsbewusstseins," and to Jung's investigations inspired by Freud on the atavistic structure of the mind, as it appears in the analysis of the archaic patterns in schizophrenia. In this way the student of primitive religion will remember the experiences of his youth—the well-known Indian games of American boys and girls—and thus expand his understanding of the primitive mind.

The person who understands is distinguished by the ability to renew and revivify continuously his own experience as well as that of the race. The great psychologists and philosophers of the seventeenth and eighteenth centuries in France and England combined the interpretation of historical events with participation in the political, military, cultural and social life of their times. We see the result in the testimonies of the understanding of the human soul given by such French and English moralists as Montaigne, La Rochefoucauld, Chesterfield, Chamfort, Hume and Vauvenargues.

All great scientists and artists need this capacity for transcending the limits of their personal experience. The great instrument for doing this is the imagination. In his book *Königliche Hoheit*, Thomas Mann has a prince ask a poet if, in order to be able to write his novel, he had had to travel around the world. The poet immediately replies, "Quite the contrary, Your Highness!" Marcel Proust calls the artist the man of Noah's Ark, who sees and understands the world from inside his ark.

The Act of Understanding

There has been much discussion in hermeneutics on the relation of the synthetic and the intuitive methods. The first operates by combining several small details to a composite picture, and the second by the immediate act of comprehension. Some have thought that the intuitive method is arbitrary, and others that without it synthetic methods can gain only partial results. We do not arrive at a complete understanding by induction, and by combination of its results, unless this procedure is accompanied by a specific act which can better be delimited than defined. We may illustrate it by comparing this specific act with the jumping of a spark between two electric poles, or with the sudden closing of a door, or with the psychological experience behind the phrase "I get it!"

Psychologists and sociologists have discussed the possibility of the direct and immediate grasp of the personality of another. Max Scheler, for one, denied all empathy and possibility of transposition. The experience of another personality is not gained by the transposition of one's own personality, for then the other personality would be obscured. Yet we anticipate and understand by wholes. That does not mean that by an act of divination we can understand another personality completely and correctly; the important thing is to seize the dominant traits of its nature. That is done by an act of comprehension in which both methods of procedure are combined. I should like to illustrate this with another phrase of Goethe's, who said that he could successfully imitate a man for an hour whom he had heard speak for fifteen minutes. The same sentiment is expressed in the sentence: "*Ex ungue leonem*" ("By the paw we know the lion.")

Once we have acquired the idea of the dominant characteristics, we may be able to understand and fit into the main context the secondary characteristics of a personality and its means of expression. Since we cannot build up the whole structure of a personality simply by understanding, we have to pick out representative features. Thus we see that to "understand" a person and his expression, means to grasp intuitively as well as to piece together many isolated observations, the salient characteristics affording clues to his personality.

We have already seen that understanding is not photographic. There is a subjective factor in it, which neither can nor should be removed. It could be asked whether a feeling of accord with a person or a phenomenon is a requisite of its understanding. Medieval thinkers dealt much with the relation between emotion and knowledge. Some of them maintained that emotion (love) is the basis of knowledge. Even such recent writers as Pascal and Scheler postulated an "*ordre du coeur*" to supplement the order of thought. Those opposed to this theory will quote the proverb which says that love is blind, a contention which is only correct if it is true that hatred sees clearly. Whole biographies have been written, prompted by the author's hatred of his subject. However, they are as unsatisfactory as those dictated by an uncritical admiration for the hero.

All this tends to prove that certain emotional factors are inclined to influence the understanding. Nevertheless, it is not so much the coloring as the presence of emotion which established the contact necessary for an understanding and for the mood in which it can be developed. There is a type of indifference which makes understanding difficult if not impossible. "*Graue, kalte Augen wissen nicht was die Dinge wert sind,"* said Nietzsche. ("Gray, cold eyes do not know what things are worth.") Yet the existence and the nature of the "affectus" have to be realized and, what is even more important, to be controlled if genuine and true understanding is sought.

We must therefore now turn to the problem of the possibility of limiting and controlling the subjective factor which we have found to be unavoidable. As a final motto for this section we may quote a word of Jean Paul—that there are three difficult things: to posses character, to draw character, and to recognize character.

The Objectivity of Understanding

The two extremes we have found to be erroneous are the notion of photographic reproduction and a radically skeptical attitude. History is not only a "fable convenue," as the skeptic would say, although occasionally we find in the historiography of our days a tendency to turn history into myth.

We can understand historical events and personalities and can check our results.

Some theories, for instance the radical theories of race, will not admit that there can be any objectivity in the understanding of another person, or of history, and if there were, it would not be desirable. It is true that not everyone can understand everything, but as we have already seen, there is the possibility of verification and control of the presuppositions on which understanding can be based. Students of hermeneutics have been much concerned with establishing objective criteria and thus defending the evidence of understanding. This procedure includes two factors, first an internal consistency in the process of understanding facts, and secondly the check which is exerted by weighing individual facts and instances against each other. Philosophical and psychological, historical and philological research and methodology have developed a great critical apparatus in order to guarantee the certainty of the evidence of the results of their interpretation.

The aim of understanding must be defined as integral comprehension, even if only an approximation to an absolutely objective understanding is attainable

I wish to repeat that such comprehension cannot be a simple copy of its object in the mind, but that it is rather a reproduction in perspective and an all-inclusive interpretation of its significance.

The Purpose of Understanding

The question of why understanding is essential has been frequently answered from a purely pragmatic point of view. I wish to call attention to another aspect of the aim of understanding, advanced by the hermeneutics of the *historische Schule*. We seem to feel within ourselves an overwhelming impulse to understand, even when no "practical" issue is involved.

"*Alles Gewesene ist wissenswürdig.*" ("All that ever existed is worth knowing"). We may add: Everything that does exist is worth knowing, though to a different degree. There are priorities in this respect which vary with the understanding individual, the period and the context in which he lives.

I cannot discuss here the interesting problem of the limits of understanding which is indicated by Nietzsche's conception of creative ability, "*plastische Kraft.*" He himself was of the opinion that nobody should be allowed to learn and understand more than he can well absorb into his personality without weakening his creative impulses. If I am right, that is the problem of our civilization and age. Should there not be a way between an indiscriminate incorporation of all and everything that our understanding can reach, and the dangerous simplification extolled by some false prophets as a return to the status "before the fall?"

Should we not try to be broad—by wide and sympathetic understanding—broad, but not shallow? We, as individuals, and as collective entities, can afford to be so, provided we have principles to guide us, when we choose and assimilate, strong but not narrow principles that will be strengthened rather than weakened by practicing understanding.

In summary we may say that the function of understanding is threefold. The first is preservation. He who understands what is and what has been, revives and preserves in the memory of men the sum of their experience. The second function is the guidance and direction of our thoughts and actions, education of ourselves and others according to the formula, *"So sollst Du sein, denn so verstehe ich Dich."* (Droysen) ("Thus shalt thou be, for thus do I know thee or thy true nature.") The third aim is to realize the scope and variety of human nature and personality, as well as its expression in all fields of cultural activity.

Notes

Introduction

1. Quoted in Thomas W. Goodspeed, *A History of the University of Chicago: The First Quarter-Century* (Chicago: University of Chicago Press, 1916), pp. 299–300.

2. See Louis Henry Jordan, *Comparative Religion: Its Genesis and Growth* (New York: Scribner's, 1905).

3. A. Eustace Haydon, ed., *Modern Trends in World-Religions* (Chicago: University of Chicago Press, 1934), xi.

4. Ibid., p. 221.

5. Ibid., p. 220.

6. Ibid., ix.

7. The official English designation is the International Association for the History of Religions (IAHR).

8. J. Wach, *Types of Religious Experience—Christian and Non-Christian* (Chicago: University of Chicago Press, 1951), xiii.

9. Notes based on these lectures were posthumously published as *The Comparative Study of Religions* (New York: Columbia University Press, 1958).

10. Quoted in Wach's paper entitled, "Research in the History of Religions" (n.d., Chicago).

11. J. Wach, *Understanding and Believing* (New York: Harper & Row, 1968), p. 107.

Master and Disciple: Two Religio-Sociological Studies

1. Tor Andrae, *Die Person Muhammeds in Lehre und Glauben seiner Gemeinde*, 1918.
2. "The power of the self-controlled, the victorious crown of the virgins, the good judgment of the once married."
3. Hans Blüher, *Die Aristie des Jesus von Nazareth* (1921); see especially chap. xi.
4. "Those who are with me do not understand me."
5. "Until the pilot tallies up the freight, he does not count the corpses who died [in the fight of truth]."
6. "Die Dioskuren," *Jahrbuch für Geisteswissenschaften*, I (1922), 35–105.

Mahāyāna Buddhism

1. I shall refer to the work by this title, which is very difficult to translate accurately—Burnouf says *Lotus de la bonne loi;* Kern, *The Lotus of the True Law* or *Lotus.*
2. Published in Paris, 1852.
3. In *The Sacred Books of the East*, ed. F. Max Müller, vol. 21 (Oxford, 1884), with a significant introduction. In quoting, I follow this translation.
4. "It might be, Ānanda, that you are therefore thinking: the Word has lost its master, we no longer have a master. You must not think this, Ānanda. The teaching, Ānanda, and the Order that I have taught you and that I have proclaimed, this will be your master when I have gone."
5. This, of course, does not mean that the apparatus of dogmatic concepts used later had already been perfected before the appearance of the Buddha and that it was only "transplanted," as it were. Such a conception ignores completely the individuality, originality, and internal coherence of historical manifestations.

6. Rudolf Otto, *Das Heilige;* the quote is from *The Idea of the Holy,* trans. John Harvey (New York: Oxford University Press [Galaxy], 1958), p. 51ff.

7. These terms are taken from R. Otto.

8. Thus in the *Lotus,* chap. 3, p. 76, the Tathāgata is the father of the world, who has obtained the supreme perfection in his knowledge of the correct means (see below) and who is very merciful, patient, benevolent, and compassionate.

9. "Upāyakauśalya"—Burnouf translates the title of the second chapter as "habilité dans l'emploi des moyens," Kern as "skillfulness." The term implies above all the discovery and application of special means—sometimes controversial (the reproach of untruth)—for saving creatures. It is "politic" in the sense of the capacity for finding the right means for the moment. Cf. *Lotus,* chaps. 2, 3, 5, 7, and 15.

10. A few of the most beautiful are that of the burning house (chap. 3), of the lost son (4), of the magic herb and the potter (4), of the magic city (7), of the jewel sewn into the garment (8), of the well-digger (10), of the crown jewel (13), and the doctor (15).

11. It is thus stressed again and again that there is in truth only one teaching (e.g., 2.68 [p. 48], 5.81–82 [p. 141]). Most of the similes are used in order to implement this idea.

12. Of course these Truths were also acknowledged in Mahāyāna. Cf. the frequent references to them in the *Lotus* (e.g., chap. 1, p. 18; 7, p. 171).

13. De la Vallée Poussin, *Bouddhisme, Opinions sur l'histoire de la dogmatique* (1909), p. 297.

14. Cf. *Lotus,* chap. 22.

15. (Editors' note.) For the remainder of the section on the ethics of Mahāyāna, Wach follows quite closely de la Vallée Poussin's article "Bodhisattva" in the 1922 edition of James Hastings, ed., *Encyclopedia of Religion and Ethics.* This schema, he says, is based on the five most important texts on the subject.

16. These are the fears of the wants of life, of evil repute, of death, of evil rebirths, and of the "gatherings."

17. *Lotus,* chaps. 8, 9, 10, 12, etcetera.

18. Walleser, *Die philosophische Grundlagen des älteren Buddhismus* (1904), p. 12.

Wilhelm von Humboldt

1. The famous linguist and psychologist Heymann Steinthal published the first treatise on Humboldt's linguistic theory (*Die Sprachphilosophie*, 1885). D. H. Brinton, the American anthropologist, followed with *Philosophic Grammar of American Languages*, 1884.
2. *Briefwechsel*, ed. A. Leitzmann (1908).

Sociology of Religion

1. For a broader exposition of the concept of the sociology of religion, as advocated here, and for illustrations from different religious faiths and groups, and more inclusive bibliography, see Joachim Wach, *Sociology of Religion* (Chicago: University of Chicago Press, 1944).
2. Cf. Henri Pinard de la Boullaye, S. J., *L'Etude comparée des religions* (Paris: Gabriel Beauchesne, 1922, 1929, 2 vols.); Simon Deploige, *The Conflict between Ethics and Sociology* (Saint Louis, Mo.: B. Herder Book Co., 1938).
3. Emile Durkheim, *The Rules of Sociological Method*, 8th ed. tr., edited by G. E. G. Catlin (Chicago: University of Chicago Press, 1938); Talcott Parsons, *The Structure of Social Action* (New York: McGraw-Hill, 1937), Part II, chaps. X–XII, and "Theoretical Development of the Sociology of Religion," *Journal of History of Ideas*, 5 (1944):176ff.
4. Lucien Lévy-Bruhl, *L'Expérience mystique et les symboles chez les primitifs* (Paris: Félix Alcan, 1938); *Les Fonctions mentales dans les sociétés inférieures* (Paris: Félix Alcan, 1928); *La mentalité primitive* (Oxford: Clarendon Press, 1931); trans. L. A. Clare (London: Allen & Unwin; New York: Macmillan, 1923); *The "Soul" of the Primitive*, trans. L. A. Clare (New York: Macmillan, 1928); *Le surnaturel et la nature dans la mentalité primitive* (Paris: Félix Alcan, 1931).
5. Arnold Van Gennep, *La formation des légendes* (Paris: E. Feauncarion, 1910); Eugène Comte Goblet d'Alviella, *Introduction à l'histoire générale des religions* (Brussels: Mozbach & Falk, 1887); *Croyances, rites, institutions* (Paris, 1911); Numa Denis Fustel de Coulanges, *La cité antique*, 20th ed. (Paris: Hachette, 1908); Paul Foucart, *Les mystères d'Eleusis* (Paris: A. Picart, 1914).

6. Raoul de la Grasserie, *Des religions comparées au point de vue sociologique* (Paris: V. Girard & E. Brière, 1899); Roger Bastide, *Eléments de sociologie religieuse* (Paris: Armand Colin, 1935); Robert Will, *Le culte* (Paris: Félix Alcan, 1925–1929); cf. also *Annales Sociologiques B. Sociologie Religieuse,* ed. Marcel Mauss and M. Granet (Paris: F. Alcan, 1939); Pinard de la Boullaye, *L'Etude comparée.* The author did not have occasion to do full justice to the modern French school of sociology of religion in his own recent contribution (note 1), because some works were not available to him.
Cf. also Robert K. Merton, "Recent French Sociology," *Social Forces,* 12 (1933):537ff.

7. Cf. Wach, *Sociology of Religion;* Max Weber, *Gesammelte Aufsätze zur Religionssoziologie* (Tübingen: J. C. B. Mohr, 1920–1921); Weber, *Wirtschaft und Gesellschaft* (Tübingen: J. C. B. Mohr, 1921), Sec. III, chap. IV, "Religionssoziologie"; Ernst Troeltsch, *The Social Teaching of the Christian Churches* (New York: Macmillan, 1931); Leopold von Wiese and Howard Becker, *Systematic Sociology* (New York: John Wiley & Sons; London: Chapman & Hall, 1932); Erich Rothacker, *Einleitung in die Geisteswissenschaften* (Tübingen: J. C. B. Mohr, 1920); Wach, *Einleitung in die Religionssoziologie* (Tübingen: J. C. B. Mohr, 1930); Theodore Abel, *Systematic Sociology in Germany* (New York: Columbia University Press, 1929); Talcott Parsons, *Structure of Social Action,* Part III.

8. *Der moderne Kapitalismus* (Munich and Leipzig: Duncker & Humboldt, 1928); trans. Nussbaum, *A History of Economic Institutions of Modern Europe* (New York: F. S. Crofts, 1933).

9. *Sociologie* (Berlin: Duncker & Humbolt, 1925); Nicholas J. Spykman, *The Social Theory of Georg Simmel* (Chicago: University of Chicago Press, 1925).

10. Wiese and Becker, *Systematic Sociology;* Wiese, *Sociology,* ed. Franz H. Mueller (New York: Oscar Piest, 1941).

11. Unfortunately Scheler's books are not translated. Cf. bibliography and discussion by H. Otto Dalke, "The Sociology of Knowledge," in Harry E. Barnes and Howard Becker, eds., *Contemporary Social Theory* (New York: D. Appleton-Century Book Co., 1940), chap. IV.

12. Cf. Alexander Goldenweiser, "The Relation of the Natural Science to the Social Sciences," in ibid., chap. V.

13. Cf. for a survey: Alfred Krauskopf, *Die Religion und die Gemeinschaftsmächte* (Leipzig: B. C. Teubner, 1935); Eva Hirschmann, *Phänomenologie der Religion* (Würzburg: Konrad Triltsch, 1940). Gustav Mensching, *Vergleichende Religionswissenschaft* (Leipzig: Hochschulwissen, 1938) was not available to the author.

14. Robert M. McIver, "Sociology," in *Encyclopedia of the Social Sciences*, 14:232–247; Ernest Barker, *The Citizen's Choice* (Cambridge: At the Univeristy Press, 1937); R. R. Marett, *Tylor* (London: Chapman & Hall, 1936); Ernest B. Harper, "Sociology in England," *Social Forces*, 11 (1932):325 ff.

15. Cyril K. Gloyn, *The Church and the Social Order (from Coleridge to Maurice)* (Forest Grove, Oregon: Pacific University, 1942); William Peck, *The Social Implications of the Oxford Movement* (New York: Chas. Scribner's Sons, 1932).

16. John MacMurray, *Creative Society* (New York: Association Press, 1936), and *The Structure of Religious Experience* (New Haven, Conn.: Yale University Press, 1936); Maurice B. Rickett, *Faith and Society* (New York and London: Longmans, Green, 1932); Vigo A. Demant, *God, Man, Society* (London: Morehouse, 1934).

17. Floyd N. House, *The Range of Social Theory* (New York: Henry Holt & Co., 1929), chap. XVIII, "The Sociology of Religion."

18. William F. Ogburn and Alexander Goldenweiser, *The Social Sciences and Their Interrelation* (Boston: Houghton, Mifflin Co., 1927); Floyd N. House, *Range of Social Theory*; Earle E. Eubank, "The Field and Problems of the Sociology of Religion," and Arthur E. Holt, "The Sources and Methods of the Sociology of Religion" in L. L. Bernard, ed., *The Fields and Methods of Sociology* (New York: Ray Long and R. R. Smith, 1934); Barnes and Becker, *Contemporary Social Theory*, especially chap. XXIII; Barnes and Becker, *Social Thought from Lore to Science* (Boston: D. C. Heath and Co., 1938).

19. Howard W. Odum, *American Masters of Social Sciences* (New York: Henry Holt & Co., 1927).

20. Shailer Mathews, "The Development of Social Christianity in America," in *Religious Thought in the Last Quarter Century* (Chicago: University of Chicago Press, 1927); James Dombrowski, *The Early Development of Christian Socialism in America* (New York: Columbia University Press, 1936); Charles H. Hopkins, *The Rise of the Social Gospel in American Protestantism* (New Haven,

Conn.: Yale University Press, 1940); Aaron I. Abell, *The Urban Impact on American Protestantism, 1865–1900* (Cambridge: Harvard University Press; London: Oxford University Press, 1943).

21. William W. Sweet, *Religion in Colonial America* (New York: Chas. Scribner's Sons, 1942); J. L. Neve, *Churches and Sects in Christendom* (Burlington, Ia.: Lutheran Library Board, 1940); H. Richard Niebuhr, *The Social Sources of Denominationalism* (New York: Henry Holt & Co., 1929). See also works cited in note 22.

22. Publications of the Institute for Social and Religious Research, especially those of Harlan Paul Douglass, Edward de S. Brunner and J. H. Kolb. Cf. also above, note 15; F. Ernst Johnson, *Christianity and Society* (Nashville, Tenn.: Arlington Press, 1935); E. W. Burgess, *The Urban Community* (Chicago: University of Chicago Press, 1925); Robert E. Park, E. W. Burgess, and R. D. McKenzie, *The City* (Chicago: University of Chicago Press, 1925); Ezra Dwight Sanderson, *Rural Sociology and Rural Social Organization* (New York: John Wiley & Sons, 1942); S. C. Kincheloe, *The American City and Its Church* (New York: Missionary Education Movement, 1938).

23. *The Catholic University of America Studies in Sociology,* especially nos. II, VI, and VII: Edward J. Kiernan, *Arthur J. Penty, His Contribution to Social Thought,* No. II, 1941; Roberta Snell, *The Nature of Man in St. Thomas Compared with the Nature of Man in American Sociology,* No. VI, 1942; W. T. O'Connor, *Naturalism and the Pioneers of American Sociology,* No. VII, 1942.

24. Robert H. Lowie, *An Introduction to Cultural Anthropology* (New York: Farrar & Rinehart, 1941); Ralph Linton, *The Study of Man* (New York: D. Appleton-Century Co., 1936); Franz Boas, *General Anthropology* (Boston: D. C. Heath & Co., 1938); Alexander Goldenweiser, *Anthropology* (New York: F. S. Crofts, 1937); Wilson Wallis, *An Introduction to Anthropology* (New York: Harpers, 1926); Eliot D. Chapple and Carleton S. Coon, *Principles of Anthropology* (New York: Henry Holt & Co., 1942); Albert Muntsch, *Cultural Anthropology* (New York: Bruce Publishing Co., 1936).

25. Otto Klineberg, *Social Psychology* (New York: Henry Holt & Co., 1940); R. T. La Pierre and P. R. Farnsworth, *Social Psychology,* 2nd ed. (New York: McGraw-Hill Book Co., 1942). Excellent criticism is given by Herbert Blumer, "Social Psy-

chology," in Emerson P. Smith, ed., *Man and Society* (New York: Prentice-Hall, 1937), chap. IV.

26. Edgar S. Brightman, *A Philosophy of Religion* (New York: Prentice-Hall, 1940).

27. William I. Thomas and Florian Znaniecki, *The Polish Peasant in Europe and America* (Boston: Gorham Press, 1918–20); cf. Herbert Blumer, *An Appraisal of Thomas' "The Polish Peasant in Europe and America"* (New York: Social Science Research Council, 1939); Ellsworth Faris, "The Sect and the Sectarian," in *The Nature of Human Nature* (Chicago: University of Chicago Press, 1938); Liston Pope, *Millhands and Preachers, A Study of Gastonia* (New Haven, Conn.: Yale University Press, 1940); Raymond J. Jones, *A Comparative Study of Civil Behavior Among Negroes* (Washington: Howard University, 1939); Arthur H. Fauset, *Black Gods of the Metropolis* (Philadelphia: University of Pennsylvania Press, 1944); J. F. C. Wright, *Slava Bohu, The Story of the Dukhobors* (New York: Farrar & Rinehart, 1940); Ephraim Ericksen, *The Psychological and Ethical Aspects of Mormon Group Life* (Chicago: University of Chicago Press, 1922); Edward Jones Allen, *The Second United Order among Mormons* (New York: Columbia University Press, 1936); Robert Henry Murray, *Group Movements Through the Ages* (New York: Harper & Bros., 1935); David Ludlum, *Social Ferment in Vermont*, Columbia Studies in American Culture, No. 5 (New York: Columbia University Press, 1939).

28. Cf. above, note 21, and William Lloyd Warner and Paul S. Lunt, *The Social Life of a Modern Community* and *The Status System of a Modern Community* (New Haven, Conn.: Yale University Press, 1941, 1942); for the non-Christian world: John F. Embree, Sure Mura, *A Japanese Village* (Chicago: University of Chicago Press, 1939), chap. VII.

29. W. F. Albright, *Archaeology and the Religion of Israel* (Baltimore: Johns Hopkins University, 1942); see also Pitirim A. Sorokin, *Social and Cultural Dynamics* (New York: American Book Co., 1937–1941).

30. See, for the following paragraphs, the references in notes 17 and 27.

31. Karl Mannheim, *Ideology and Utopia*, p. 256.

32. Edwin E. Aubrey, "The Holy Spirit in Relation to the Religious Community," *Journal of Theological Studies*, 45, 1940.

Radhakrishnan and the Comparative Study of Religion

1. *My Search for Truth* (1937, in *Religion in Transition;* sep. offprint, 1948), 19.
2. E.g., *Eastern Religions and Western Thought* (1939).
3. *East and West in Religion* (1933), Lecture I.
4. *Ibid.,* 32.
5. *Eastern Religions and Western Thought,* 306.
6. *East and West in Religion,* 36.
7. *Ibid.,* 36.
8. *Ibid.,* 19.
9. *Die Absolutheit des Christentums.*
10. But cf. the chapter on "Islam and Indian Thought" in *The Heart of Hindusthan* (1936), 65ff.
11. *The Religion We Need* (1928), 24.
12. Christianity is, after all, an "Eastern" religion. Cf. *East and West in Religion,* 46.
13. *East and West in Religion,* 38.
14. *Idem.*
15. *Idem.*
16. *Nature, Man and God,* 315.
17. *East and West in Religion,* 47, 57ff.
18. *Ibid.,* 58.
19. *Idem.*
20. Cf. the chapter "Christendom I" in *Eastern Religions and Western Thought,* esp. 163ff., 176, for Dr. Radhakrishnan's answer.
21. *Eastern Religions and Western Thought,* 314.
22. *Ibid.,* cf. 316f., 324.
23. *Ibid.,* 314.
24. *Ibid.,* 316f., but cf. 319.
25. *Ibid.,* 320.
26. *Ibid.,* 324.
27. *Ibid.,* 326.
28. *Ibid.,* 343.
29. *Ibid.,* 344.

30. *Ibid.,* 345ff.

31. *Ibid.,* 345.

32. *Ibid.,* 347.

33. *The Heart of Hindusthan,* 88.

34. Wach, J., *Types of Religious Experience,* Chap. II.

35. *The Heart of Hindusthan,* 101.

36. *Ibid.,* 102.

37. In his book, *Types of Religious Experience, Christian and Non-Christian* (1951), the author of this paper has attempted an analysis of the differences between the Christian and the Mahayana-Buddhist faith. Cf. Chap. VI.

38. *Nature, Man and God,* 97.

39. *The Heart of Hindusthan,* 103f.

40. *Ibid.,* 165.

41. *Ibid.,* 104.

42. *Ibid.,* 109.

43. *Ibid.,* 109, 121.

44. *The Reign of Religion in Contemporary Philosophy* (1920), 287.

45. *Ibid.,* 122.

46. "The Place of the History of Religions in the Study of Theology," *Journal of Religion,* XXVII (1947), 157ff.; cf. also *Types of Religious Experience,* Chap. I.

47. *The Reign of Religion in Contemporary Philosophy,* 275.

Index